# THE CRAFT OF
# WRITING ARTICLES

**Other Allison & Busby Writers' Guides**

# THE CRAFT OF WRITING ARTICLES

*Second, revised edition*

Gordon Wells

a&b

This edition published in Great Britain in 1996 by
Allison & Busby Ltd
179 King's Cross Road
London WC1X 9BZ

First published by Allison & Busby 1983
Reprinted, 1984, 1985, 1988, 1989

Copyright © Gordon Wells 1983, 1996

The moral right of the author has been asserted

A catalogue record for this book is available from
the British Library.

ISBN 0 74900 298 0

Designed and typeset by N-J Design Associates
Romsey, Hampshire
Printed and bound in Great Britain by
WBC Book Manufacturers Ltd
Dridgond, Mid Glamorgan

# CONTENTS

# INTRODUCTION

So you'd like to write for magazines and newspapers? Good. It's a great occupation. If you will work at it you will surely succeed. There is always room for another new writer.

You will sell your work to editors: your words and thoughts will be read with interest by thousands of people. Your literary efforts may – perhaps – be less artistic than your friends' pottery or paintings, but they will be far more widely appreciated. The achievement of publication is every bit as welcome as the satisfaction gained from any other creative craft. And you will know that your work is good enough to sell in an open, competitive market.

And anyone can do it. You don't need to be a literary genius – that could indeed be a disadvantage. You don't even need to have done well at English in school. Editors are more interested in good ideas than beautiful phrases. (Like writers, editors are as likely to be women as men, but for convenience I have referred to both editors and writers throughout in the third person as "he".)

The surest way of getting into print in a magazine or newspaper is to write feature material: not the short stories or poems favoured by some as "more creative", but hard factual articles. The demand – the market – for articles is far greater than for short stories. Taking a random sample of magazines from the racks and counting only the obvious 'outside' contributions, there are at least four times as many articles as stories. (The sixteen publications that I looked at comprised seven women's magazines, six general interest magazines and just three "technical" magazines. If all published journals were to be considered – with the preponderance of specialist magazines that there is – the ratio of articles to stories would probably be nearer ten to one.)

And poetry has little chance of achieving paid magazine publication at all.

## A paying hobby

To emphasize the point already touched on above, one of the benefits of article-writing is that it is a paying hobby. The cash outlay is small; the rewards can be large. The annual *Writers' & Artists' Yearbook* lists over six hundred magazines published in Britain that accept and pay for factual articles. Most of these magazines rely on freelance contributors supplying them with material: if the supply were to dry up, these magazines could not continue for long. And the yearbook is not a complete list of all the magazines open to the freelance writer; many small or limited-interest magazines, which are often very good markets, are left out.

It is not easy to quantify the financial side of article-writing. It is, after all, a market-place in which we are operating. Editors may pay more for a particularly interesting article than for a more run-of-the-mill one. Payment too will often depend on the editor's assessment of the author's fame (if any). A magazine with a large circulation will usually pay more than one with a small circulation. But a glossy prestigious magazine will often pay less than a more popular "down-market" paper. And usually, of course, a longer article earns more than a short one.

There are British magazine that pay hundreds of pounds for an article of perhaps two thousand words. There are others that pay no more than a few pounds. (For many years – well into the 1990s – the quarterly *Bedfordshire Magazine* has even offered payment of just £1.05 [an old-fashioned guinea] per thousand words. They surely can't attract many good contributors.) Freelance writers supply material at both extremes of payment. The great majority of articles at present seem to be paid for at about £50-70 per thousand words. Certainly, year on year, the *average* of my own payments for articles is around that figure.

Writing in English means that magazines elsewhere in the world are also open to the British freelance writer. American magazines, particularly, often pay very high rates for material suited to their specific needs. But overseas markets require special study and should not be attempted until a writer is already successful in the home market.

Whatever the rates of payment though, the principle is the same. My work – and yours too, if you are prepared to work at it until you are successful – is worth buying. Each editorial acceptance is a 'prize' in the ongoing writing competition.

The purpose of this book is to explain the craft of article-writing as an enjoyable and paying HOBBY. It is, of course, possible to make freelance article-writing a full-time occupation: but this is not a practical proposition for most people. It is *not* what this book is about. For many years, I wrote articles for magazines in my spare time, after putting in a full day's salaried work – plus several hours of daily commuting-time. This book is based on my years of part-time writing experience. (I am no longer a wage-slave; I now work full time at various writing activities – of which article-writing is only a fairly small part.)

I made money from writing articles in my spare time, and I had fun doing so. So too can you.

## What it takes

Having determined that you want to write; that the openings for articles are better than for other forms of writing; and that you can make money at writing; let us look at what it takes to be an article-writer.

Three qualities particularly are needed to make a success of article-writing:

- some ability to write,
- an enquiring mind (and usefully, but not essentially, a seeing eye),
- a professional approach.

## Writing ability

If you can write a 'newsy' letter or advise your neighbour on the best way to prune his or her roses, you can write an article. It doesn't matter a bit that you were never any good at writing 'compositions'or essays at school. Article-writing is not a particularly *literary* exercise. Clarity is far more important than 'Quality'.

Having said that, it is nevertheless essential that you enjoy – or can grow to enjoy – stringing words together. And one of the best ways of learning to string words together is to see how others do it – by reading. Read widely, and catholically.

Read the English classic novels and read – particularly – the daily tabloids. Read the articles that others write about 'your' subjects, and read 'pulp' novels. And always, as you read, study how the words are put together. Notice how the tabloids favour short, easy to read, sentences: note the beauty – and sometimes the 'heaviness' – of many classics and the soporific effect of many learned articles.

Note, particularly, the lengths of sentences and paragraphs, and the complexity, or otherwise, of the words. In Chapter 5, where we look at the actual writing process, I advise you to keep sentences and paragraphs short and words simple. This is fundamental.

No one can really teach you how to write though. In this book I offer guidance on what has worked for me. An 'on the spot' teacher might perhaps correct faults, but only you can write your own words in your own way. However you write, if you hope to sell, write so that it is easy to read: think always of the reader. Abandon any literary pretensions and put aside all delusions of literary grandeur. Your aim, as an article-writer in search of paid publication, must be to write interestingly – not impressively. And simplicity and clarity come from using short, everyday words and short sentences.

## The enquiring mind

The ability to write in a way that will interest readers springs from what can best be called an 'enquiring mind'. Just as a young child absorbs information by asking seemingly incessant questions, so too does an article-writer develop interesting subjects.

The article-writer reads a tiny snippet of news or information and ponders on it:

- Why did this happen?
- Is this the first time?
- What was the cause of it?
- Who did it first?
- When?
- What will come next?
- Where did that come from?
- How was it made?
- Can it be done again?

... and so on.

Chapter 2 considers how article ideas can be developed from such pondering.

The ordinary reader reads, and having read, moves on. The article-writer stops. Automatically, he wonders whether he can write an article about anything that interests him – and he is interested in almost everything. This is one of the side benefits of article-writing as an occupation: it broadens your interests; it can make you a more interesting person. When the article-writer is interested in a subject he will write interestingly about it – and interesting articles are saleable articles.

As already remarked, editors are not particularly concerned about writing style – their needs are simpler. They want articles to be interesting, original and easy to read. Accuracy is taken for granted; if your work is found to be inaccurate, it will be a long time before you sell the next article. And humour is a rare bonus.

An article on a topical subject will almost always be of interest. A successful article-writer will often be able to provide a topical tag for an otherwise straightforward general interest factual article. Such tags are of greatest importance when submitting articles to daily newspapers.

## The professional approach

We have just noted that editors expect the work being offered to them to be easy to read. This perhaps exemplifies the professional approach to article-writing. If your work is to sell it must be written with that object always in mind. Think of who is to read what you write. You are writing for the 'average reader' of a specific target magazine. Don't write to please yourself: write to attract and interest the magazine-rack-browser. If you write for yourself, you could find yourself the only reader – and that is both pointless and profitless.

The successful article-writer assesses the likely reader of his work. Then he writes in a way which THAT READER will find easy to read. Chapter 3 explains how to assess the typical reader of a magazine and Chapter 4 discusses how to use a typical article as a 'model'.

But there is more to producing a saleable article than the mere writing. Indeed, the actual stringing together of the words is little more than about twenty per cent of the craft of article-writing. If you are to write with the object of selling your work – and thereby having it read by thousands of people throughout the land – you must undertake a more comprehensive routine.

From start to finish the whole article-writing process entails:

- getting an idea for an article (or, even better, for a set or series of articles) – about twenty per cent of the process;
- investigating the subject, collecting material, etc. – about thirty per cent of the whole process;
- determining suitable markets for the article(s) – an essential twenty per cent of the process;
- writing up the material – amounting to little more than about twenty per cent of the job;
- preparing and presenting the article to the editor, and keeping records and accounts – the final ten per cent.

The first three components listed above – the idea, the subject research and the market research – are closely interlinked. Often an idea will come first. But an idea is not enough on its own: it has to be an idea suitable for a specific market. And unless there is enough material available to produce an article, an idea is of little use. Sometimes, ideas spring directly from market research. Similarly, subject research is an ongoing process which often generates ideas.

It is best to think of the idea, the subject research and the market research as three inseparable and interrelated parts of the process. All three components are essential prerequisites of the writing and presentation processes. In all, they account for some seventy per cent of the article-writer's activities.

Adopting a professional approach to article-writing also entails being business-like. Any good businessman seeks to maximize his productivity and minimize his outlay; applying these principles to article-writing means we must look more carefully at the three components discussed above.

If you can sell several different articles on the same general subject you can reduce the effort per article on subject research. One outlay of research time means that only the remaining seventy per cent of effort is needed for subsequent articles. As an example, I have written several times, for different markets, about unusual hats. Latterly, if I find a new market, I need do no more than merely update my basic subject research.

Similarly, writing a series of articles for a single magazine does not entail repeated market research; an ongoing awareness of any significant changes in the magazine's general approach is all that is needed. Writing a regular column for a magazine is a way of economizing on more than twenty per cent of the effort – for the selling too is already done.

The actual writing of each article is work that cannot be reduced. Indeed, anyone who enjoys their work would not wish to avoid the task of choosing the words, stringing them together and then the polishing of the final result. In Chapter 5, without laying down hard and fast rules about the very personal craft of writing, there are useful guidelines – rules of thumb – for simple, easy-to-read writing.

And the final, ten per cent, part of the professional approach to article-writing is the preparation and presentation of your work to the editor. You are seeking to sell your wares. So present your work in the form that editors require. Basically, this means that it must be in typescript, double-spaced, on one side only of A4 paper. If you don't present your work in this way it will usually not even be considered. There is no way to buck the system. Further details of the presentation of your work are contained in Chapter 7.

## The seeing eye

There is a further aspect of the article-writing craft which has to be mentioned. Some subjects lend themselves to, or positively call for, being illustrated. Freelance article-writers who can provide their own illustrations for such articles will improve their chances of selling – and increase their income.

Modern cameras are relatively cheap and surprisingly simple to use – despite their sometimes complicated appearance and the almost inevitable surrounding jargon. Any reasonably intelligent person willing to read a simple instruction book can take photographs of an acceptable technical standard to accompany a general interest article. And, as with literary prowess, artistic ability too is barely necessary. Similarly too, pictures intended for publication are best if simple, uncluttered and clear. These qualities are achieved, almost automatically, by moving in close to the subject.

A further benefit from cultivating a seeing eye, to complement the writer's enquiring mind, is that article ideas can themselves be generated from pictures or sets of pictures. Rather than the usual couple of illustrations to accompany an article, it could be that the *article* is written to accompany a set of illustrations. Any such extra activities can only be to the writer's advantage. Chapter 6 looks into the whole question of illustrations for articles – how to make them and how to present them.

## Getting started

There is one further aspect of freelancing – not really article-writing, but closely akin to it – that is *not* dealt with later in this book.

And that is writing 'Letters to the Editor – intended for publication.

Many publications welcome letters from their readers and pay for all that are published; others pay only for the 'star' letter. The payments may look small, but in terms of payment per thousand words – the normal freelance measure of payment – letters are often surprisingly well paid for their fifty to a hundred words.

The skills in writing such letters are: to be amusing, interesting, or provocative; and to make every word count, within a limit of about a hundred or so words. It is an ideal first market for the amusing personal experience or anecdote. It is an ideal training ground for the would-be article-writer. (And other people's letters are a good source of article ideas for you.)

Another advantage in trying to write 'Letters to the Editor' is that they need not – indeed, should not – look professional. They need not be typed, as long as your writing is legible. And they can be on 'ordinary' notepaper. The letters should look as though they were written out of altruistic interest and/or conviction, rather than with the express objective of seeing one's work in print and earning a few pounds.

For those wishing to pursue writing 'Letters to the Editor' there is an excellent book in this series: *How to Write Five-Minute Features* by Alison Chisholm – who regularly earns hundreds of pounds a year from 'Letters'. And an up-to-date list of paying 'Letter' markets is included in each edition of *The Magazine Writer's Handbook*.

Some magazines will also publish – and pay for – a single photograph on their 'Letters' page. Sometimes this will be on its own and sometimes illustrating a letter which, itself, may not be paid for. These magazines are thus good markets for intereresting single pictures; I have sold a number of photographs merely by writing short unpaid letters about them.

## The writer's life

Finally, in this introduction, a word about the life of an article-writer. Writing is a lonely activity. No one can join you in staring helplessly at the word-processor screen or blank sheet of paper.

Few people can really help you in developing ideas – although some may unwittingly spark them off. The way you string your words together is your responsibility. You are on your own.

There are, of course, advantages to the solitary nature of the article-writer's occupation. You can write a first draft almost anywhere, ignoring those about you. You can always utilize those delays and hold-ups that are an inevitable part of modern life to think of ideas, openings, titles and anecdotes. (But make a note of your thoughts before they fade; I have forgotten innumerable marvellous ideas through omitting to write them down at the time.)

Whenever I am waiting for a train I browse through the magazines in the station bookshop. This serves as 'initial sift' market research: it helps me to decide which magazines are worth buying for detailed study. And – within reasonable limits – I never mind waiting for the dentist or the doctor to catch up with my appointment time. I spend the time studying the unusual magazines in the waiting-room.

But it is all too easy for the article-writer to become lonely. You can get to feeling that no one else is suffering the same agonies of word-choice or waiting anxiously, like you, for the editors' decisions. To reduce such loneliness, try joining one of the many Writers' Groups or Circles. Ask at your local library for details of your nearest Writers' Circle, or consult Jill Dick's *Directory of Writers' Circles* – see Appendix. Most circles meet regularly for helpful talks or discussions – and you get to know other writers.

A few words of caution though, about writers' groups. Beware the circle which is a social, rather than a working gathering; beware the circle where literary *creativity* takes precedence over writing for publication; beware too, the blind leading the blind – check that at least some circle members are regularly achieving (paid) publication. These warnings apart, a good, working writers' circle can be of immeasurable benefit to a lonely beginner.

Another way of easing writers' loneliness is to subscribe to one of the several writers' magazines now available (see Appendix). No matter how good you are at writing, or how frequently or easily you sell your work, you will always pick up some useful hints from these magazines. And you will find that most of your worries are common to other writers.

From the magazines too, you will get to know of the several marvellous writers' conferences, workshops and 'schools' that are held annually. There are few things more stimulating to a writer than to spend a weekend or more in the company of dozens of other writers – all bubbling with enthusiasm.

You return to your lonely desk, enthused. You're not alone.

The more you write, and the more regularly you write, the better your writing will become. And above all, don't be discouraged by rejections slips – every writer gets them. Good, successful writers are the ones that keep trying. You WILL succeed.

# WHAT TO WRITE ABOUT

In order to write you must have something to write about. This is obvious. Without a subject – something to say – the only recourse is to copy out the telephone directory, or whatever. And that won't sell: telephone users get their directories issued free.

What do you need for a subject? Clearly you need something that will interest the potential readers – and as many of them as possible.

What, then, are people interested in? You can best answer that question by asking it of yourself. What are *you* interested in? And the answer will almost always be – in differing order perhaps – your job, your hobby, your home, your family, your health, your holiday, or just something unusual and/or interesting – including 'interesting people', well-known people, 'personalities'. Just as you find these subjects interesting, so too do most other people. The list covers a wide range of subjects, and the more interesting the subject you choose, the easier it will be to sell your article.

## What do you know?

It is also obvious that, even when you have decided on a subject, you must know something about it. It would be simple for me to say that I was going to write an article about, say, growing strawberries in a window-box. That might indeed be a good subject for an article, but I couldn't write it – because I know nothing about growing strawberries. It is a subject likely to attract popular interest yet unusual enough not to have been done to death by other writers. But you must know your subject before you can write about it.

The first golden rule for article-writing can therefore be stated:

## ALWAYS WRITE ABOUT WHAT YOU KNOW

Ask yourself, what do you know most about? The answer will usually be your job, your hobby, your home, your family relationships, your holiday and odd things that you find unusual and/or interesting, including interesting people. In other words, the same list of subjects that other people are likely to be interested in.

Unless you are connected with the medical profession the ever-popular subject of others' health is best passed by – at least initially. (When you are a well-practised article-writer you can consider writing such personal-experience health articles as 'How I cured my pneumonia by standing on my head in the snow'. Before writing such articles though, think first whether you have something inherently interesting and unusual to say to others. Or are you merely indulging yourself – or even just carping? If what you have to say is not really unusual, then a doctor will say it better. There are plenty of writers in the medical profession. And the editor will buy a doctor's article about health matters in preference to yours every time.)

The same qualification about the need to say something really unusual and of general – rather than personal – interest must also apply to writing about family relationships and holidays. Few people outside your own family circle are likely to be interested in what you said to Aunt Martha when she broke one of your best wine glasses, or how you got lost in Majorca. Make it really witty and they might – but we can't all be humorists. (Even if we think we are.)

### Subjects of interest

We are therefore wise if we initially restrict our writing to hard, factual information about our work, our hobbies, things around the house and garden, and any subjects – including travel – that are of particular and unusual interest. In fact, to subjects about which we have some knowledge that is worth imparting.

Another factor to bear in mind when selecting individual article subjects is that most people are interested in people – that is, the human aspects of any subject. An article packed with nothing but dry factual information will be just that – dry. Add an anecdote or relate the facts to their impact on ordinary people and the article springs to life. (Bringing 'life' to an article is further considered, in detail, in Chapter 4; my purpose here is merely to emphasize the interest of people in people.)

In choosing a subject to write about, think about what might interest other people in your job or hobby. An accountant could, perhaps, write a short article about how to avoid paying tax on family gifts, or how to support one's offspring through college; a housewife on preparing the garden produce for freezing, or how to cook left-overs in the microwave oven; a painter and decorator on how best to paint window frames – without painting the glass; an amateur meteorologist on the facts behind the 'red sky at night' and other forecast bases.

There are many job-related possibilities – but they are not endless. The wise writer broadens his horizons.

### Specialist subjects

To be successful as a writer of articles it pays to be interested in as many things as possible. A successful article-writer is a person of catholic interests. Yet, to paraphrase an old saw, *a little knowledge is an insufficient and potentially embarrassing thing*. Make yourself knowledgeable therefore – a mini-expert – about a limited, but ever-increasing, number of matters of interest. A catholic interest broadens the field from which you can select subjects for your articles.

Now we can expand the scope of our first golden rule – it is no longer enough merely to *Write about what you know* but:

## GET TO KNOW YOUR SUBJECT WELL BEFORE WRITING ABOUT IT

We'll call this one Rule 1A.

But how are you to select the subjects into which to expand your interest? This must vary from person to person but perhaps I can helpfully illustrate the idea. By profession I am/was a civil engineer, concerned with highway planning (I now think of myself as a 'lapsed' engineer); this led me, deviously, to an interest in street furniture in general, and articles about street lights in particular. My wife and I once lived in Asia, as a result of which we collect oriental antiques – and I have written a number of articles about them. While abroad, I became interested in the unusual hats of the Borneo peoples – back in England I have written about these and all sorts of other curious hats.

I also became particularly interested in dragons: I have seen and photographed dragons in China, in London and even on the roof of a shop in central Brighton; I have collected a treasure-chest of fascinating information about dragons. As a result, I've written several illustrated articles about 'my' dragons.

Most of all, I have developed my interest, and modest success, in writing, to actually writing and lecturing on writing techniques.

In thinking about subjects in which to specialize, it is worth considering the amount of popular interest they are likely to attract. But also bear in mind that a good writer can make almost any subject interesting, by the way in which he presents his material.

One well-known British freelance writer collected postmarks and wrote about them for many years in a wide variety of seemingly inappropriate magazines. An article illustrated with the postmarks of such quaintly-named American towns as Smokeless (Pennsylvania) and Coke (Virginia) sold readily to the specialist *Gas Times*. It all depends on how interesting you can make your subject – and how well you aim your article at the specific reader.

## Article ideas

But a subject on which you are knowledgeable is not necessarily enough. You need the specific idea for the article. The idea is really just what to say about one of your subjects.

A painter and decorator could perhaps write *volumes* about 'painting' – but magazine articles are seldom more than a page or two long, and need correspondingly briefer subject ideas. He would do better with the short article suggested above – on painting window-frames. This is a little snippet of a subject, just right for an 800-word article. (Chapter 4 expands on the question of fitting article subjects to article lengths. There are few worse writing faults than a subject too big for the article's length.)

The problem is to generate an ongoing stream of ideas for articles. Ideas are to the article-writer as petrol to the motor-car: neither can do without. Some ideas will spring to mind as soon as you start to think about writing. Others will well up unbid at inappropriate times, sparked off by a chance remark. Ideas for new articles will be generated by reading magazines dealing with your interests. However, wherever and whenever an idea comes to you, note it down: ideas are notoriously transient. Keep a notebook – an Ideas Book.

Study lots of magazines – pay attention to the ideas that other writers have developed. Try to recapture the published writer's thought process. Why did he write that article *in that way*? What made it interesting to the editor (who bought it) and to you, the reader (who also bought it)? Can you apply the same thought process to your own collection of subjects? (The consideration of sold articles – the writer's market research – is developed further in the next chapter: at this stage we are only thinking about how ideas are developed.)

Old magazines too – picked up in junk shops or at jumble sales – are worth studying. You can often safely 'borrow' an idea for a new article directly from an old one that sold – and the older the better. You will only be taking the basic idea and some of the facts. The way you present your updated article will be fresh – and your own.

There is no copyright in ideas, facts or titles, only in the way they are presented. (See also Chapter 8.)

## 'Brainstorming' for ideas

Another way of generating article ideas is what is sometimes known as 'brainstorming' – mental doodling. Take anything – an abstract thought or a trite saying; an animal, a vegetable or a mineral; or a manufactured item – and ask yourself questions about it. How was it made? Where does it come from? What does it mean? Who first said it? Who invented it? What can be made from it? How do we eat it? What does it eat? The questions keep coming; the answers generate further questions. By this process you can always produce ideas for not just one, but several articles. I have never known it to fail.

The questions spring from a standard 'origin': the journalist's/ reporter's fact-seeking fundamentals. One-time newspaper-man Rudyard Kipling lists them memorably:

> I kept six honest serving men
> They taught me all I knew
> Their names are What and Why and When
> And How and Where and Who.

With my technological background I usually remember them as 5WH: five Ws (Who? What? Why? Where? When?) and an H (How?).

It matters not how you remember them, but remember them you should. They will prove an invaluable and never-ending generator of article ideas.

Suppose you are walking along the beach; you notice some seaweed – in which you have long been vaguely interested. (I haven't.) Seaweed?

- What do you know about seaweed? 'Start by consulting a dictionary and an encyclopedia.'
- Does it only grow in the shallows? (It depends on how you define 'shallows'.)
- How far out to sea does it grow? (I was so interested that I've just had to look it up: to about 200 metres depth of water.)
- Does it need air? Or light?
- How many different types of seaweed are there?
- Can you eat it?
- Isn't there something called *laver bread* that is made of seaweed? (The dictionary says *laver* is edible seaweed but it doesn't mention laver bread.)
- Where do they eat it? (Somewhere around Liverpool – I think. Or is it Cardiff? Can this be checked? Where?)

17

- Don't the Japanese eat seaweed? (I recall buying cocktail canapes from Japan, in the supermarket. They were flavoured with seaweed.)
- If it is edible, is it 'farmed'? If not, why not?
- Isn't seaweed sometimes used as manure?
- Is there any connection between seaweed and ozone? (Seaside towns used to suggest so.)
- Is it the ozone that seaweed smells of? In any case, why *does* it smell?

The answers to just those questions, together with the further questions that spring to mind as you discover the initial answers, might well make an interesting factual article. I deliberately posed the questions as quickly as I could write them down and without prior thought, to illustrate the method. You could do the same.

Indeed, why not have a go right now? Explore the background, origins, *raison d'etre*, etc., for: paper tissues, the several UK one pound coins, the ubiquitous duvet ... you name it. You can hardly fail to become interested as more and more questions spring to mind. You may have already generated an idea for your first/next article.

## Developing the ideas

The experienced article-writer thinks beyond the single immediate idea though. To discover the answers to the seaweed questions will involve quite a lot of research – which is discussed later in this chapter. But a lot of research for a single article can easily be uneconomic, if only in terms of your time. It is better to be able to use the one lot of research for several articles.

Let us look again at the idea. It is in fact not yet an article idea; it is no more than a collection of interesting snippets of information for possible future use. These need to be collected, collated and fitted together interestingly – *interestingly*.

Assuming that the answers justify the ideas, articles along the following lines could all be prepared from this one research exercise:

- 'Why don't we eat more seaweed?' – a short and provocative (paid for) letter for a family magazine or a daily newspaper, in summer. Also perhaps suitable for a South Coast local newspaper in summer when they are likely to be plagued with seaweed.
- 'Your fertilizer grows – under the sea' – explaining how some ferlizers are derived from seaweed. For a farming magazine.
- 'Eat seaweed – live longer' (or – grow slim, or ...) – a filler for a general or family magazine.
- 'England's only/first/oldest seaweed farm' – for an agricultural or 'county' magazine.
- 'Snorkelling through the farmyard' – a lightly factual, possibly futuristic, article about the food value of seaweed for the children's pages of a Sunday colour supplement, or for a children's magazine with an educational bias. Also – a similar article, but re-slanted, for a women's magazine, tied to the holiday season.
- 'Fat-free/Vegetarian food from the sea' – heavier, more factual article for a popular scientific magazine and/or for a vegetarian or other health food magazine.
- 'Forgotten underwater shrubberies' – with underwater photographs perhaps, for a natural history magazine; possibly even for a photographic magazine.

Think how much more readily you could have generated a set of article ideas from within your own areas of interest. And remember: the more you know about your own interests, the less additional research you need to do for any one batch of ideas.

It will be noted that each of the articles suggested in the above list is associated with a type of magazine. Before any of the articles were written, this association would be focused down to a single magazine as a 'primary target'. The article would be written specifically for the target magazine. The days of a general article 'suitable' for a wide range of magazines, and sent on from one to the other as each in turn rejected it, are long gone – if they ever existed outside of rose-coloured false memory. Articles should be written for specific magazines – as is further explained in the next chapter.

As an article idea evolves – or comes to you in a flash – write it at the top of a fresh sheet of paper. Express the idea as a working/tentative – and for you, a helpfully reminding – title and

suggest a possible market. Then, over time, while you are looking for the content material, try to develop the one basic idea into
ideas for several articles, as above. Build up a file of ideas – your
Ideas Book. With such an Ideas Book (or file) you will seldom if
ever need to ask yourself what to write about next.

## Ideas not worth following up

Take care though. There are some article ideas that – usually –
you should reject even before you start. Check your ideas against
this list of 'Don'ts':

● Don't write critical or spiteful articles – unless you can do it
  extremely cleverly or wittily – and probably only then if you've
  already got an editorial go-ahead.
● Don't write humorous articles (nor try to inject weak witticisms
  into an otherwise serious article) – unless you really are funny.
● Don't write *obvious* 'reference book' articles – the editor's
  staff can probably do it better and cheaper.
● Don't write about *your* holiday – help me with *mine*.
● Don't write about medical matters – medical experts can do it
  better.
● Don't write about the obvious *anniversaries* – someone else
  will have got in first (or they'll already have been done to
  death).

## 'How-to' articles

Another type of article, basic to every writer's repertoire, is the
'How-to' feature. If you can *do* something – make a cigar-box vio-
lin, grow strawberries in a window-box, paper the ceiling without
papering yourself, anything – you *know*. And if you really know
how to do something, and if it is something of interest to others,
you can write about it and probably sell the article.
   With that one qualification – that it is something of interest to

others – there is a seemingly open-ended market for 'How-to' art-icles. (You may be expert at sterilizing empty jam-jars or making a cut-out doily from a £10 note, but these skills, while possibly laudable, are hardly likely to interest a multitude of readers.) More than any other type of article though, the 'How-to' article often needs supporting illustrations. If you have not got, and cannot get, photographs or drawings of your DIY activities at various stages, you may find it less easy to sell a practical 'How-to' article.

It is not unreasonable to categorize the travel article as a spe-cialized form of 'How-to' article. We have already emphasized the need for an article about holiday travel to be more along the lines of telling the reader how best they can enjoy their own experi-ences rather than one solely describing the writer's experiences. But, of course, the best way to guide the reader is often to describe what you have done yourself. It's all a matter of the way you say it; the *attitude*.

Everyone wants to write an article about their latest holiday; the competition for acceptance is therefore often fierce. The best advice for budding travel writers is to study the masters: the travel writers whose columns appear in the quality dailies and the more prestigious magazines. Cathy Smith's *How to Write and Sell Travel Articles*, in this series, is a particularly good introduction to this specialism.

But DIY or travel, the 'How-to' article is perhaps the only type of factual article which needs virtually no further research – beyond engaging in the activity being described. All other types of factual article depend on *research*. What does this mean to the article-writer?

## Research sources

Research, to the article-writer, means the collection of factual material. A squirrel – could squirrels write – would be well equipped to be an article-writer. I have already mentioned – in the first chapter – that article-writing is something like 20 per cent writing, 10 per cent presentation, 20 per cent market research, 20 per cent ideas and 30 per cent research. Research is clearly of considerable importance. The article-writer does not have to advance the frontiers of all human knowledge – indeed this could often be a disadvantage. The role of the article-writer is more to bring useful information together and present it in an entertaining and interesting way to the layman.

The article-writer derives his factual information from, in random order of importance and of ease of acquiring:

- an encyclopedia
- books on the subject
- other articles on the subject
- newspaper news stories
- press releases, from large firms and government departments
- free brochures and similar hand-outs
- educational material – explanatory leaflets, educational supplements/features in newspapers (notably *The Guardian*), etc.
- advertisements
- personal observations
- anecdotes recounted to him
- personal interviews
- personal notes taken from radio or TV programmes, or from lectures
- museums
- reference libraries
- correspondence (and/or phone calls) with useful and interesting people – 'contacts'
- answers to specific queries addressed to embassies, government departments, large firms, etc.

And even that seemingly never-ending list is almost certainly incomplete.


## Research – books

An encyclopedia is always a good place in which to start your research. As soon as I started musing to myself about seaweed, above, I looked in two single-volume encyclopedias – the

Macmillan and the Penguin – always in instant reach above my desk. It was in these books that I discovered that seaweed grows not only in the shallows but also out to 200 metres depth of water.

I also possess a set of Everyman's Encyclopedia which, after mention of laver bread and the use of seaweed as a fertilizer refers the reader to the entry on the seashore – which in turn lists a number of reference books. Every would-be article-writer should have at least one encyclopedia: I recommend the Macmillan one as probably the best.

Were I really interested in the flora and fauna of the seashore I would undoubtedly already possess – as I do for many subjects that do interest me – at least one or two simple *introductory* books about them. Useful series of such books include:

- the Hamlyn *Little Books* – colourful paperbacks, many may now be out of print but they can perhaps be picked up second-hand. (I notice, from the back of one which I do have, that they publish one called *Seashores* and another called *Life in the Sea*. These might well have more on seaweed – if you're really 'hooked'.)
- the Warnes *Observer's Guides* – on a wide range of subjects.
- the various Shire Publications' series: *Discovering* books and *Shire Albums* in particular.
- the vast range of Penguin books – on virtually every subject under the sun.

And, often – wrongly – forgotten, children's books, particularly:

- the still inexpensive Ladybird books – on history, foreign countries, how things work, etc. Again, many of the ones on my shelves are now out of print but can often be picked up second-hand. (*The Ladybird Kings and Queens of England* is always my first source for the important events in any reign – but it obviously wouldn't help with seaweed.)
- the newer, *Funfax* and other series (*Know Alls*, etc.) published by Henderson Publishing – many are jokey, but there is a vast amount of information in these 'pocket-money' books.

Depending on the depth of my interest in a subject, I would have other general reference books. Reflecting my own interests, I have a number of books about important dates (the Penguin *Chronology of the Modern World* for example), about history (most but not all of the 9-volume *Pelican History of England*), about dragons, and about superstitions, to mention just a few of 'my' subjects.

Clearly, one is also well-advised to check what is available from second-hand bookshops and from those shops and mail-order firms specializing in reduced-price 'remaindered' new books. And of course, the local library will usually have an appropriate book that can be borrowed.

## Research – newspapers and magazines

Equally, over time, I would almost inevitably see one or two articles about seashore aspects – if not on seaweed exclusively – by other writers. Preferably, I would extract these articles from the magazines and retain them. If not, photocopy them.

Similarly, in perusing my daily newspaper, there will be little snippets of information about all sorts of subjects that interest me. Not just seaweed, for that idea has only just come up, but anything of present or potential future interest. I cut them out, mark them with the source and date (most important, this), and retain them. And don't neglect advertisements. On occasions, there are whole series of advertisements containing information on subjects peripheral to and sometimes even remote from the advertiser's product. I collect these too. (Some years ago a major overseas bank ran a series of advertisements about unusual types of money: from cowrie shells to Chinese 'shoe' money. I collected these ads and made good use of them. And there was also – some while ago – that delightful series of Shell advertisements about the countryside.)

The importance of newspaper cuttings to an article-writer is hard to over-emphasize. These little snippets of news update more learned books and articles: they also include bits of light relief ignored by the more learned, but which are *manna* to the article-writer.

Akin to press reports and advertisements are the hand-outs, press releases and free brochures often available from the most unexpected sources. At one time, London Transport issued a vast selection of brochures describing things to see and do, places to visit, in and around London. No doubt they still do – but nowadays they probably charge a small fee for the more useful. Similarly, tourist offices and banks used to offer tourist brochures about London; whenever you see anything of this nature – for free – snap it up. Much of the content will not date.

Don't overlook the one- or two-sheet descriptive leaflets produced for tourists/visitors by the major museums; these are seldom expensive and are frequently ideal for the article-writer. The article-writer doesn't always want *all* the information there is; a summary often suffices. (And I would certainly see what the Natural History Museum in London had on seaweed.)

The reference, and general non-fiction sections of major public libraries – and perhaps university libraries too, if you can gain access – can of course be most valuable sources of information. Certainly you could expect the major libraries to have available most of the reference books listed in encyclopedia items. And don't forget the British Library Newspaper Library at Colindale, London NW9: all British newspapers published since 1800 are stored and available there.

Of major importance to the article-writer too – but often overlooked – is the facility whereby your local library can obtain scarce books for you, on loan, from any other library anywhere in Britain. I have never yet found my library unable to get me any book that I have needed. Try them. (You'll find that most librarians will go to considerable lengths to help anyone wanting something slightly more serious than the newest Aga-saga or thriller. Mine's marvellous.)

## Research – people who know

The enthusiastic – and successful – article-writer does not limit his research to published material though. He will go out and seek first-hand information, information not yet recorded elsewhere – by talking to people and asking questions. Who knows, there may be a professor of oceanography living in the next street; or even just a seaweed collector or enthusiast. An enthusiast is almost certain to be willing to talk – at length – about his favourite interest.

And, moving away from the example of seaweed research, the concept of talking to people leads us into the world of interview articles.

The public seems always to be interested in the lifestyle, views, experiences, backgrounds, etc of well-known people. And interview articles are a fruitful area of work for the experienced article-writer: I only qualify that comment because a beginner is unlikely to win an interview with a 'name' personality.

You need to work your way up the scale. Leaving aside the big names, there are still plenty of opportunities for the beginning article-writer to interview interesting people: I have seen interviews of 'ordinary' – but interesting – people like the manager of an old people's home, the owner of a successful one-person business, or those who have triumphed over some physical adversity, featured in major magazines. As long as there is an interesting story there, magazine editors can be tempted.

There is detailed advice on how to interview the famous and the 'ordinary-but-interesting' in Sally-Jayne Wright's book *How To Write and Sell Interviews* in this series.

But reverting to interviews as a research tool for a factual article: they are of immense value to the article-writer. The information will be direct from the horse's mouth; it may well be as yet unpublished; it can – particularly if encouraged – be well-larded with personal anecdotes which will bring potentially dull facts to life in your article. The only hurdle to overcome is your own nervousness. Your nerves aside, your 'quarry' will almost certainly be delighted to help you.

A worthwhile precaution is to ensure that you have some sensible 'start-up' questions, to get the interview going. You must not make too big a fool of yourself – i.e. display total ignorance – in the opening minutes; once the conversational ice is broken and a rapport established, this is no longer so important.

It is not advisable to make prolific notes during an interview. Continuous scribbling can put a nervous person 'off their stroke'. Note down the odd key fact – 'Do you mind if I just make a note of that?' – but otherwise rely on your memory until you leave the presence. The moment you are out though, write down everything that you can recall.

26

A portable cassette recorder, with built-in microphone, can be a helpful tool: but again, some people find them inhibiting. (In my experience, most people find a separate microphone more 'off-putting' than a built-in one.) Only use a recorder if the inter- , viewee is perfectly willing and wholly unconcerned. And, as with any mechanical device, check it before you start interviewing: fresh batteries, fresh cassette – and spares in case the interview runs on.

(I once arrived to interview someone, intending to over-record on a used cassette – only to discover that I'd broken off the little plastic over-record protection nib on the cassette. Luckily, I quickly saved the situation by filling the gap behind the broken-off nib with balled-up paper. It worked, but I've never made that mistake again.)

A useful tip for when you are collecting material by interviewing people for research information is to build up 'information chains'. Near the end of each interview, ask your 'victim' if he can put you in touch with anyone else, to take you further with the subject: obviously though, out of politeness, ask for someone specialising in a slightly different aspect of the subject. This often pays off, or a name may be mentioned in passing, which you can pick up on. Don't forget to ask for the address, or at least, a telephone number.

## Research – letters

Of importance perhaps second only to personal interviews is information acquired by personal correspondence. If you hear of, say, an oceanographer living on the other side of the country, a personal visit may not be possible. You can write or you can phone. I always *prefer* to introduce a question in writing even if I then follow up with an interview by phone. A written introduction enables the interviewee to prepare. And a written reply to a specific question is much less ephemeral than a phoned response. I like letters.

But a letter seeking information needs to be better prepared than, for instance, the preliminary notes for a face-to-face interview. You can't 'feed' on the answers. It is non-productive to ask general

27

rambling questions, the answers to which are in any standard reference book. Ask detailed, personal and specific questions and you will usually get back detailed, personal and specific answers – unless you were getting too personal. Success is even more likely if you enclose a stamped envelope clearly addressed to yourself.

Foreign embassies, government departments and large firms too will almost always answer specific – relevant – questions most helpfully. Address the queries to the Public Relations Department or Press Office (PRO) at the head office of the organisation. You can find most of the addresses from the London telephone directory; if you live remote from London, your local library will have the directory. Nowadays, even when writing to large firm or government departmental PROs, a stamped addressed envelope is usually a sensible precaution: the absence of one will sometimes mean no reply at all. (And regrettably, even the provision of a reply envelope will not always, these days, guarantee a response.)

Finally, in this review of research sources, don't forget: the wealth of information transmitted daily by the broadcasting and television companies (and particularly the lectures of the Open University); the proliferation of adult education evening and weekend courses open to all; the lectures and talks given in major museums – often in the lunch break – by leading experts; and of course, the 'one-off' lecture in the village hall. Attend, or switch on – and absorb – anything that looks remotely interesting. Make prolific notes – no one will be put off and speakers will be pleased by your zeal.

## Notes

Notes are an important part of an article-writer's stock-in-trade. Notes should be made from borrowed books, after personal interviews, after (or, if you are very good, at) talks and lectures, and of personal observations.

Note-taking methods are a personal matter, but there are a few essential characteristics. Notes must:

● identify name – and qualification – of source, and date of note-making. (For notes from borrowed books the source should include book title, author, publisher, publication date, the source from whence you borrowed it, and often the page number in the book. The ISBN (International Standard Book Number) – usually found on page iv in the preliminary pages of a book – is also a useful thing to record: it will help any librarian to identify and get the book.

- be well spaced – to enable you to annotate or amend them later.
- be set out so that their content is both clearly identifiable and easily read.

(My own practice, in respect of the last two points is, at least when making hand-written notes, to write blocks of notes on alternate half-widths down a page, and with several lines between each block.)

- as far as possible, be restricted to one subject per page – for later ease of referencing.
- be accurate – of course.

Do not overlook – in making notes from book – the possibility of photocopying a key diagram. One such illustration can often be as good an *aide memoire* as several pages of hasty notes.

Similarly, as a supplement to your notes of what that village street or native girl *looked* like remember to use your camera. Even if, despite today's 'any-fool-can-do-it' camera-simplicity, you still can't take a saleable photograph, your 'happy snaps' will always help to jog your memory. A quick snap will also save you having to write down all the information on the nearby plaque or notice. Carry your camera with you whenever you are 'working'. (See Chapter 6.)

## Research storage and retrieval

But what good is your widespread information gathering if it is all in a jumble? Next to none. A good writer 'squirrels' his research material away with care. Right from the start, file away your cuttings, your photocopies, your articles torn from old magazines, your written notes, in a tidy and logical fashion.

It is a good idea to stick small newspaper clippings on to sheets of A4 paper, several to a sheet – and preferably all on the same subject. Small cuttings get lost more readily than A4 sheets; and even these, I find, have a habit of 'putting themselves away' in the most inappropriate places.

I make, or transpose, all of my written notes on lined A4 paper, ready-punched for filing. Similarly, all word-processed notes are printed out on A4 sheets and hole-punched. Most letters from PROs, press notices, etc., are also of A4 size. So too are all photocopies and most torn-out magazine pages. It is easy to standardize all research material on the A4 size: it simplifies filing – and retrieval.

My own practice is then to keep all papers relating to one subject in a large, A4-sized, document wallet, the subject being clearly marked on the top flap. Within the wallets, sub-divisions of the subject are kept in clear plastic folders. But this is more costly than it need be; for many years I used recycled A4 envelopes for subject files and occasionally grouped subjects together in a few document wallets. The greater sophistication came with a (marginal) increase in affluence.

As a collection of material gets too much for one recycled envelope, clear plastic folder or overall document wallet it can readily be split down further into associated files. I have a large number of envelopes, folders and wallets – but it's easy to sort throgh the contents of any one. When I come to write an article, I extract the relevant sheets from one or more envelopes to work from. (And – usually – they get back into the right envelope/ folders.)

Another, more sophisticated, way of storing research material for easy retrieval is to file everything in A4 lever-arch files as it is collected. Each sheet is numbered consecutively – and a running list of page contents maintained on the top of the file – and the files lettered alphabetically. The essential complement to the files is then a card index. You would open a card for each new aspect of each subject in which you are interested; on the card, note the file and page number of each appropriate sheet of notes, cuttings, etc. This method is more efficient than mine. Were I starting today from scratch I might well adopt it, but I am 'too far gone' with the multi-envelope/folder system to change now.

However you store your material, be sure that it is a logical and expandable system *that you can live with*. You NEED to be able to find facts quickly and easily.

But always remember that you are a WRITER – not a 'fact-filer'. It's the end product that's important, not how you got there.

## Sets

Finally, your research collecting and storage will be particularly valuable if you can collect *sets* of information. Six snippets of news information about unusual hats is of more immediate value than six snippets about six unrelated subjects. The six hat items could well be enough, together with your basic general hat knowledge, to make a brief article.

The collection of sets is particularly relevant to the camera-owning article-writer. An illustrated article written around pictures of half-a-dozen unusual gates, or door knockers, or bridges, or street lights, or ... will always sell. But see Chapter 6 for advice on what best to photograph.

You will again have noted the emphasis in the last two paragraphs on the unusual. Collect information about, or pictures of, the unusual: the *usual* is commonplace and won't sell; the *unusual* is uncommon and therefore interesting, and will always sell. And if the unusual is also amusing, so much the better. (I have long treasured the news item from which I learnt that the name of the Catholic Cardinal of Manila is Sin – making him Cardinal Sin. But so far I have not yet found a use for this, to me, amusing piece of information.)

# 3

# WHO TO WRITE FOR: MARKET RESEARCH

Having by now decided on a subject you feel competent to write about and duly researched it, you need to think about where to sell your article. Yes, that too comes before the writing. If you don't know for whom – for which market, or magazine – you are writing, how can you write to meet their special needs?

As an illustration of the importance of deciding on your market before you write the article, think of two extremes. Imagine, if you can, an article on, say, seaweed (again) in *CHAT* or *New Woman* and a similar article in *Country Life* or *New Scientist*. It is obvious that, while the general subject matter just might be of interest to any of these markets, the treatment would be vastly different. The article for *New Woman* might be titled – and written along the lines of – 'Seaweed can affect your sex life' or 'Daily seaweed ends bedroom boredom'. In a more sedate magazine the same (imaginary) facts might be graced with a 'Bio-medicinal properties of English algae' title. The way in which the facts – and the conclusions – were written up would differ greatly.

If you look at books about freelance article-writing published fifty or so years ago, they will probably suggest writing a 1000-word general interest article and then 'sending it on the rounds' of supposedly suitable magazines. That might have worked then ... but I doubt it. It certainly will not work today. Articles today need to be written with a specific market in mind. Nowadays, there are far fewer general magazines and many more specialist journals.

But writing with a market in mind does not necessarily mean that this is the only market for which your article is suitable. It merely means that this is the market at which you are primarily aiming. If you fail to sell to the first target magazine, it may still be possible to sell to a secondary market. See below.

## Markets for beginners

So, which magazine shall you write for? Many a tiro thinks initially of writing for a national daily, the *Readers' Digest*, or a weekend colour supplement. And this is wrong.

Your object, as a beginner, is to get your work into print, for pay. (Avoid working for nothing: if your work is worth publishing, someone will pay you for it.) If you try to write for the big-paying prestige markets while you are still learning the craft, you will be up against competition from the experts. There are many skilled freelance writers who make a large part of their living from writing feature articles for the 'big' magazines. You've got to effectively 'serve your apprenticeship' first.

My advice is therefore, initially, to seek out the lower-paying markets: smaller magazines and local publications. The experts will be less interested in writing for such markets and therefore the competition should be less. But remember that tiny fish still taste sweet to all of us; there will still be *some* competition. The lesser competition does not mean that the quality of your work can be anything less than your best. The lower-paying markets are an excellent training ground – their standards are as high as any.

Another approach to choosing a market is to consider the number of 'sales opportunities' it offers.

A quarterly magazine made up of a dozen or more freelance contributions may be a better market than a monthly with only two or three freelance contributions per issue. Consider:

4 x 12 = 48 purchases per year by the editor of the quarterly;

12 x 2 = 24 purchases per year by the editor of the monthly.

But don't be misled by this example. Not all quarterlies take more material than all monthlies. Check the opportunities for yourself; check, too, the rates of pay – where you can. (See below.)

Still on the broad principles of choosing a market, there are other factors to be taken into account. Although I advise against submitting your early work to the big national dailies, that advice does not apply to the regional press. Like the nationals, the regional dailies often feature freelance work in 'children's pages', 'weekend leisure pages', 'money pages', etc. They often also take general interest articles *with an appropriate regional flavour* for their feature pages. And the emphasis in the previous sentence is most important. Regional dailies are as parochial about their area as are the nationals in respect of London activities and interests.

And don't forget the magazines that you yourself take regularly. If you have read *Amateur Gardening* from cover to cover each week for the last few years, you are already well ahead in market research. You KNOW what sort of article *Amateur Gardening* wants; you KNOW what the average reader wants; you ARE, in all probability, the archetypal average reader. And by now you probably know a fair bit about gardening. You will be able to

## WRITE ABOUT WHAT YOU KNOW.

Which, of course, is the first *golden rule* for article-writers.

### Choosing your market

You cannot afford to take many magazines regularly over long periods though. You can't be the typical average reader of every magazine for which you aspire to contribute. You must select and study your potential markets in other ways.

Browse around the shelves in your local newsagent – railway and airport terminal bookstalls are even better, they are used to people killing time – and identify interesting-looking magazines. Consult the CURRENT edition – out-dated editions are *worse* than useless – of one or other of the major writers' yearbooks:

*Writers' & Artists' Yearbook* (A. & C. Black, annually)
*The Writer's Handbook* (Ed: Barry Turner, Macmillan/PEN, annually)

In them, look at the Classified Index of publications to identify those in your own areas of interest; work through the main alphabetical list of magazines and newspapers. Identify those that look likely to interest you – or be interested in the subjects on which you are knowledgeable.

The yearbook entries are helpful but brief. They will say something like:

**Phone-card Collecting** (1993), Joe Bloggs, Gemini Publishing plc, 75 Sunset Boulevard, Muddlecombe, Muddlesex MU9 95X *tel* (01222) 999800 *fax* (01222) 999801.
£2.95. M. Articles of interest to phone-card collectors. All contributions must appeal to the specialist collector, general interest features are not required. *Length*: up to 2500 words. *Payment*: on acceptance, by arrangement.

The date is that of the magazine's founding; the name is that of the editor – address editors by name whenever possible. And if no name is given, try phoning the editorial office and asking the telephone operator/receptionist/secretary for a name. The price is that of the magazine which is shown as a monthly.

The rest of the information is of only limited assistance to the not-yet-knowing freelance writer. There is not enough detailed information about the type of article preferred and its 'slant' or 'approach', to guide the writer; there is insufficient information about the readership 'level'; the length requirement is so vague that it tells us nothing. And the payment advice is, as so often, unhelpful.

Every two years, I research and describe, from an ordinary freelance writer's viewpoint, a small, carefully selected group of general interest magazines for *The Magazine Writer's Handbook* (Allison & Busby, biennial). In this I identify the typical readership, list examples of recent articles used with titles and lengths, give up-to-date information on how the magazine prefers to be approached, and always at least some idea of how well or badly they pay. My *Handbook* looks specifically at the magazines most likely to publish non-specialist general interest articles by freelance article-writers.

But with all reference books there is inevitably a time-lag between research and publication. In some respect or other, albeit as minimally as possible, they're all bound to be out of date the day they're published.

More up-to-date market information for the article-writer is available, in varying degrees, in the monthly writing magazines, *Writers' Monthly* and *Writers News/Writing Magazine*. Even more current information is available in the specialist newsletter, *Freelance Market News*. (For details, see Appendix, page 133.)

But even backed up and updated by *Freelance Market News*, the yearbooks or *The Magazine Writer's Handbook* can only give the article-writer the basics. Before submitting work, the writer must always still study the magazine itself.

And there are other magazines.

## Lesser-known and specialist magazines

The two yearbooks each list several hundred British publications – and many overseas markets. My *Handbook* offers details of less than a hundred magazines. There are hundreds of magazines not listed – usually because they are too small or too specialized to offer many opportunities to the freelance writer.

But often, as suggested above, these small and/or specialized magazines are just the ones the tiro writer should aim at. Within your specialism or occupation you will know, or can get to know, the small specialist journals. (And don't ignore the many free magazines – most pay their writers, and often well.) The prudent freelance writer also spends time looking *regularly* at the magazines on display in newsagents. The magazine world is in a permanent state of change.

It is not only in the lower-paying magazines that the competition from other freelance writers is lessened. Within each specialist interest/occupation there can only be a limited number of the freelance article-writing population operating. A skilled sailor might be able to write about sailing but many other freelance writers could not; surely, only a dedicated phone-card collector or lace-maker could write knowledgeably about the fascination of phone-cards or lace; few article-writing doctors (and there are many) could write for a civil engineering magazine – and vice versa. Similarly, living in Sussex, I am unlikely to be able to offer many articles to, for instance, the Yorkshire *Dalesman* or *The Scotsman*. And again, vice versa – I hope.

Wherever you go, keep your eyes (and ears) open for little-known new-to-you magazines; don't forget to note the strange magazines in doctors' and dentists' waiting-rooms. Keep up-to-date by reading the market reports in the writing magazines – and *Freelance Market News*.

## Samples

Having identified a number of magazines – and perhaps newspapers – as potential markets for your work, you need to obtain sample copies of them. Yes, copies, in the plural – not just one. And they need to be right bang up to date, not ancient jumble-sale copies.

Before you dash out to buy all these samples though, pause a while. How many are you going to get? I could go through all the steps I have outlined above and sort out several dozen potential markets for myself. But could I *cope* with that number of markets? Certainly not, at least initially.

Suppose I *were* able to write one acceptable article for each of the thirty to forty markets I have selected. When could I write the next one for the same market? It is far better to build up a steady relationship with a few editors than to provide a lot of editors with 'once-only' sales.

Advantages of building a relationship with any magazine are:

- Knowing your work has been good in the past, the editor will tend to look favourably on each new submission from you. (But only while you keep up the same acceptable standard of reader-interest and writing-quality.)
- When the editor needs to commission a special article, your name may come to the editorial mind. (Having had one two-part article accepted plus a couple more submitted on spec and still being considered, the editor of a magazine, otherwise new to me, phoned to commission an article. [*See* 'Hallowe'en', Chapter 5.] The subject was new to me, which meant some frantic research. But it was a sure sale from out of the blue – and a struggling article-writer can't afford to look a gift horse in the mouth. It also had the bonus of opening up a new subject for me.)
- Your overall work is reduced by the need only to update your market research. (Remember the breakdown of freelance article-writing into: idea, 20 per cent; subject research, 30 per cent; market research, 20 per cent; writing, 20 per cent; presentation, 10 per cent. Repeated selling to the same magazine changes these figures to something like: 20, 30, 5, 20, 10 – a saving of fifteen per cent of the overall effort. And

a commissioned article obviates the need to think up an idea: a saving of a further twenty per cent.)

For your first efforts therefore, narrow your choice of 'target magazines' down to just two or three. If possible, let these be totally different types of magazine. Ideally, choose one or two magazines that accept general interest articles and one or two dealing with your special interests. (More than one specialist magazine only if you have more than one specialism – not two on the same subject.)

These two or three targets permit you to think of two or three different articles; which can, of course, be different treatments of the same subject. Restricting yourself to two or three magazines keeps down the cost – and the not inconsiderable effort – of market study.

Buy two or three current and sequential copies, or every other issue, of your finally narrowed-down choice of two or three magazines. Not all the magazines of your choice will be on sale at book stalls. In such cases, write to the editor – a typed, businesslike letter – explaining that you hope to write for him and asking for two or three recent sample copies. Ensure that you enclose sufficient payment to cover cost and postage. (If you're lucky, you might get the samples for free – but don't count on it.)

If you have to write for samples, it is also worth taking this opportunity to ask if the magazine has a 'contributors guide' that you can be sent. (Only a few British magazines offer such guides; many American magazines offer comprehensive writer-guidance brochures.)

Only when you have produced one or two saleable articles for each of your three initial targets, should you think about researching alternative markets. Search then for magazines with requirements as similar as possible to each of your initial targets. You will not always find such markets. When you do though, they can be offered articles that you are quite sure are saleable, but which have been rejected by your initial target magazine.

(Notice that, in the previous paragraph, I say 'produced saleable articles for' rather than 'sold articles to'. You must ensure that your articles are of saleable standard/quality – but they may still be rejected, for all sorts of reasons. This can happen if an editor has recently run an article on your subject;

however good your article is, it would then be rejected. Only occasionally will editors tell you the reason for their rejections.)

## What to look at

You now have to *get into* the magazine of your choice. Not 'be published by' at this stage, although that is your end objective, but *get into the mind* of the editor. For what sort of reader does the editor produce the magazine? Your object will be to write what that reader wants, and expects to read, in that magazine. That is what the editor will buy. Editors have a very clear picture of their typical reader – age, sex, interests, level of affluence, geographical location, family relationships, etc. The successful freelance article-writer develops a similar picture.

You must also try to determine how much of the magazine's contents is the work of freelance writers, and how much is staff-written.

The first things to look at when studying a magazine as a market for your work are not the articles themselves, but rather:

- the advertisements,
- the contents page, and
- the illustrations.

## Studying advertisements

Advertising is a highly sophisticated profession. The advertising agencies know just who are the readers of each magazine in which they display their clients' wares. They will, if necessary, vary their product presentation – their advertisement – to suit the readers of a particular magazine. By studying the advertisements the writer can work backwards to an appreciation of the reader at whom they and the magazine are directed.

Take the *Amateur Photographer* for example. There are few advertisement in the *AP* for home film-processing kits. There are many advertisements though, offering commercial processing of films. This seems a good indication that most *AP* readers are not much interested in developing or enlarging their own film and pictures. I question whether an article on film processing would sell as readily to the *AP* as one on, say, how to freeze the movement of a passing racing car – or 'suggest' speed by not freezing it. (That's not to say that from time to time the *AP* doesn't run processing articles – merely that you might have a better chance with one on picture-taking techniques.)

Back to general principles: don't look merely at the whole-page advertisements. Look carefully too at the small 'single-column-10cm' boxed advertisements, usually grouped together as a 'Market Place' or similarly titled page. Some magazines even have a 'Job Market' section which is particularly useful to you. The sort of person they are advertising for is often the typical reader.

Advertisements for personal stairlifts clearly indicate an older reader. Similarly advertisements for 'Stop your child's bed-wetting' suggest a family readership in the twenties to thirties age-range. Building society advertisements too can be helpful – they can be directed either at older income-seekers or at young mortgage-deposit savers. Either way, they tell you something about the readership.

Note particularly – but do not automatically shy away from – magazine that contain either no advertisements at all or only single-product advertisements. These may be house magazines, still sometimes – less often these days – produced just for the prestige or as vehicles for 'company policy' statements to staff.

Similarly, don't overlook airline in-flight magazines and the like. They may have few advertisements but they often welcome *knowledgeable, well-targeted* freelance articles.

Apart from the contents of the advertisements, it is worth looking at their quantity. Free magazines, which have proliferated recently, rely wholly on their advertisers for their livelihood; the editorial matter may be little more than a 'come on' for the advertisements. Minimal and/or poor editorial matter will, however, eventually be self-defeating; readers will not bother to read it – or the adjacent advertisements. The better free magazines pay well for editorial material, to ensure a welcome for the magazine and a noticing of the paying advertisements.

But no editor with a lot of advertising, whether his magazine be free or expensive, will be prepared – or allowed – to upset his advertisers. An article 'knocking' a product or type of product represented in the advertising pages will seldom be accepted – no matter how good the article may be. Save such thoughts for consumer-research publications.

## Studying editorial pages

Consider next the Contents page of a magazine. Frequently this will separate out for you the regular columns from the special features. Regular columns – either staff-written or a long-standing series written by a regular freelance expert – come under a variety of headings. They can be called, simply, 'Regular Features', 'Departments', 'Regulars', or even just 'Also'. They may sometimes be identifiable in the list of contents by their being the only items without a writer's byline or an explanatory sentence.

It is important to take note of the regular features because these deal with areas of interest where you stand little or no chance of selling your work. If an editor is committed to buying an article every week/month/quarter from an expert on, say, money matters, he is unlikely to buy one from you on family budgeting. (I have occasionally fallen into that trap myself – failing to recognize a column as a regular feature.)

The Contents page will also identify the amount of fiction the magazine carries. In the context of selling articles, the pages devoted to fiction are lost to you. But the story titles may offer a further indication of the magazine's readership.

The titles of articles too, and the accompanying 'blurb' tell you something about the readership. Are the titles flamboyant, brash and 'pushy'? Are they overtly sexy, or just suggestive ... or fairly staid? Are they down- or up-market (i.e. in tabloid or broadsheet style)?

Even the space and importance devoted to the Contents page is of interest. Some magazines restrict or omit altogether the contents listing: their readers are unlikely to bother to read it. The readers are probably regular buyers of the magazine and like to dive straight in. They know what to expect. These magazines – *CHAT* springs immediately to mind as an example – sell by action-packed internal pages and an attention-grabbing cover. Other magazines, designed perhaps for slightly more serious-minded readers, attract purchasers through their Contents pages. The computer magazine *PC Plus*, for example, is of that type; its list of contents often spreads over about four pages.

Leave now the Contents pages and flip through the rest of the magazine – looking at the pictures. Photographs of beautifully-prepared food dishes on elegantly laid tables might suggest an up-market middle-aged female readership. Pictures of scantily-clad girls suggest a readership of around-twenty-year-old girls – or men of any age. Pictures of expensive cars, exotic far-away places and a mix of well-preserved older people and young children, all in the same magazine, suggest a readership of fairly affluent grandparents. (*Choice* is an example of such a magazine.)

Thus, you can quickly get a feel for a magazine's readership – from the advertisements, the Contents page, and a quick flip through the illustrations. Now turn to the articles themselves.

## Studying the articles

By sorting out the staff and regulars' features from those supplied by freelances, you have considerably reduced the work of studying the articles themselves. At this next stage in the market-study process you want to look into:

- article subject – in a generic rather than specific way. (Thus, not 'Interview of TV megastar Billy Bloggs', but just 'personality interview'. Billy Bloggs himself is not important; the editor is unlikely to want another article about him for some while.) Identify personal-experience articles, travel features, How-to features, etc.
- article length. Count the words in ten full lines; count the number of lines in a full column free from headings or illustrations. Divide the number of lines by ten and multiply the result by the words in the counted ten-line passage. (Example from a random magazine lying on my desk: 54 words in ten lines; 85 lines

in a full column – which was hard to find. 85/10 = 8.5; multiply by 54 words = 459 ... which I would round off to 450 words per full column.)

Use this figure as a first, rough basis for estimating overall article lengths by assessing portions of a full column, allowing for illustrations, crossheads, etc. A word of warning though: column widths and hence words per ten lines can often vary considerably within the same magazine; make sure that your ten-line count is relevant to the article being looked at.

While counting words, get a *feel*, too, for the lengths and numbers of paragraphs in some of the articles. The more popular magazines tend to prefer shorter paragraphs – and sentences too – than the more up-market, serious magazines. (We shall come back to word counting in more detail in Chapters 4 and 5.)

• article illustrations. Check the number of pictures accompanying an article. Were they essential to the sale – as in a photo-feature – or merely there to liven up the page? (The latter were probably put in by the editor.) Look for bylines on the illustrations crediting the writer, or on the article itself, saying something like 'Words and pictures by Joe Bloggs'; these indicate that the article-writer offered the editor a – sometimes essential, always attractive – 'package deal'.

How much colour is used? Notice how many illustrations are upright and how many horizontal – and how many include, or are of people. (Again, we shall return to the subject of article illustrations in Chapter 6.)

You will notice that even now we are not really studying any one article in great detail. We come to this in the next chapter, where we pull to pieces an article chosen as a model.

## A market-study example – *My Weekly*

To exemplify the approach recommended above for studying a magazine, let's look at one issue of *My Weekly* (This is a realistic target magazine for tiro article-writers, published by D. C. Thomson & Co – who have a reputation for dealing well with beginners. They won't tell you how to do it, but if you're 'nearly there' they'll sometimes offer encouragement.) And don't forget: it is not enough to study just one issue of a target magazine.

This study of *My Weekly* is the same exercise as I undertake every other year when preparing each new edition of *The Magazine Writer's Handbook*. The only difference is that here, I'm including all the details (other than about the fiction) and explaining my working methods. Do remember too, that I don't *know* any editorial details: everything reported here is my interpretation, based solely on careful observation; you can – and must – do just the same thing for yourself.

I don't need to read what the *Writers' & Artists' Yearbook* says about how old *My Weekly* is: I can tell from the front cover. The issue I'm studying is number 4254: with 52 weekly issues per year that makes it well over 80 years young. A well-established journal.

Issue number 4254 has a bright, cheery-looking cover with the face of an attractive young woman smiling at me. Surrounding her are three more colour photographs relating to what's inside.

There are 56 pages including the front and back covers. Of the 56 pages, 10 are 'proper' advertisements and 4 more are 'advertorial' – editorial type material relating to and 'recommending' various goods for sale. The advertorial pages are under such titles as 'Shopping Centre' and illustrate giveaway products – foods, beauty products, etc.- alongside offers for sale. One double-page spread illustrates various swimming costumes citing chain-store availability and prices. In addition, there is a one-and-a-half page 'feature' offering a *My Weekly Bargain* tapestry set.

The conventional advertisements can be broadly categorized, by pages, as:

| | |
|---|---|
| Food | 1 |
| Clothes (including shoes) | $1^1/2$ |
| Collectables (plates for the wall, etc.) | 2 |
| Aids for the disabled (stair-lifts, electric wheelchairs, recliners, etc.) | 2 |
| Finance (savings, loans, etc.) | 1 |
| 'Next week's issue' and other D. C. Thomson publications | 2 |
| Odds and ends | 1 |
| | $10^1/2$ pages |

From the review of advertisements – supported by the magazine's sub-title *The Magazine for Women Everywhere* – it is clear that the target readership is women, which is no surprise. The limited amount of food advertising, the tapestry special offer together with the disabled aids and finance adverts suggest a mature, say 50-year-old, readership. But this view is counterbalanced by the one clothing advertisement which shows a woman of about 30: a conclusion supported by the fashion page and some of the other advertorial offers. It's probably safe to say that the readership ranges from 25-year-olds to young 60-year-olds. It is also important to note an overall impression that the 'affluence level' is somewhat 'down-market'.

Now to the Contents – it occupies a mere half-page. Top of the listings is the fiction. This issue has one episode of a serial (extracted from a best-selling book), one story in an on-going series, and three complete short stories. In all, about 15 pages (over 25 per cent) are devoted to fiction; fiction is important to the readers of *My Weekly*. And then there are the Features and Regular pages.

There are regular columns/pages relating to: health (2pp), the countryside (1p), book reviews (1p), pets and pet-care (2 $^1$/2pp), recipes (5$^1$/2pp) and a crochet pattern (3pp). As well as these, there is a Problems page and a Letters page. In all, 17 pages – and with only two exceptions, none of these are suitable pages for the freelance article-writer to contribute to.

(The exceptions are the Pet page – which contains what appears to be a short freelance contribution and also several readers' pictures of their pets – and of course, the Letters page. Paid-for Letters to the Editor are a useful field in which even the most inexperienced of article-writers can achieve publication. (See Chapter 1.) The study-issue of *My Weekly* includes 8 letters, the longest – also the Star Letter – being less than 200 words long and most being no more than 100 words. *My Weekly* currently pays £3 for all letters published and gives a valuable prize – in this issue it was a feature-packed BT phone – for the Star Letter.)

The 'non-Regular' features are of more importance to the freelance. They occupy nearly six pages in all – more than 10 per cent of the whole magazine. In the study-issue there is: a 'personality interview' with two TV 'soap' stars; a lavishly illustrated feature interview with a lady who collects pomanders; an illustrated 'How-to' feature on flower arrangements (extracted from a recently published book); and a 'Your Own Story' feature. (There is also a half-page devoted to readers' poems – but this need not concern us here.)

All the 'non-Regular' features (and the regular columns/pages too) are illustrated in colour only, with the exception of the 'Your Own Story' page, which uses a black and white photograph.

It's likely that all of the 'non-Regular' features I've listed were produced by freelance article-writers. The TV-soap-star interview however was probably pre-agreed and commissioned by the editor. For this, the editor would almost certainly go to a freelance whose work he already knows. The 'How-to' feature was probably 'placed' by the book's publisher. The most immediately interesting features are the interview with the pomander collector and the obviously reader-contributed 'Your Own Story'. Make a note of these for possible detailed study.

But remember: our purpose, *at this stage*, in looking at the magazine's contents is still primarily to build up a picture of the typical reader; to assess the magazine and what the editor wants.

The characters in the stories tend to be in their early thirties – or younger. Certainly several of the illustrations show younger characters. The 'non-Regular' features are about mature ladies. The Problems page contains questions from a young single mother and a 60-year-old grandmother. Throughout, we still have the wide range of readership shown up in the advertisements. *My Weekly* seems to be all things to all people – with a broad spread of readership.

The readership picture is made more clear by the features pages: there is a strong emphasis on home-building – mouth-watering recipes, crochet patterns, flower arrangements, pets, etc. The article about the pomander collector reinforces the same image, as do the advertisements for decorative hang-on-the-wall collectors' plates. A mature home-owner.

I have, I think, developed a good idea of the sort of article that can be sold to *My Weekly*. I'm also sure I know the typical reader well enough to write for her. (When writing for *My Weekly*, I would picture in my mind a 'young-in-heart' 40-year-old woman reader.)

Don't forget though, when doing this market-study exercise for yourself, you need to dissect more than a single issue of your target magazine; studying two or three consecutive issues will make it easier to separate the one-off freelance contributions from the regulars'.

One thing I haven't done is comment on the lengths of the potentially freelance contributed articles. Both the pomander article and the 'Your Own Story' feature are about 800 words long. Most *My Weekly* features are written in an easy-to-read style: short words, short sentences and short paragraphs are the rule. But for more on writing style and a more detailed appraisal of a single 'model' article, see Chapters 4 and 5.

## Sell to the editor

And now, before leaving the marketing side of freelancing, let us look at the buyer. (Never forget, as an article-writer, you are SELLING – into an increasingly hard, buyers' market.) The buyer is not, as far as you are concerned, the reader; your buyer is the editor. He buys what he believes his readers want. But if the editor changes, often, so too will the buyer's policy.

Picture then the editor, who has to produce a magazine, without fail, every publication day; he has so many blank pages to fill – juggling the balance of advertisements, ilustrations and text. He probably couldn't, and certainly doesn't want or intend to write all the material himself. Nor has he sufficient full-time staff to write it all for him. So he buys work from freelance writers.

Once it is known that an editor is in the market to buy articles, he will be inundated with material. Much of it will be totally unsuitable. (Too many unsuccessful freelance writers do far too little market research: it's arguably their greatest fault – offering irrelevant material.) Therefore, when an editor does find fresh, interesting material, geared specifically to his needs, he seizes on it. He builds up a stockpile of suitable material.

When the editor starts to plan the next issue of a magazine, he starts with his regulars: features and fiction – which often occupy the same pages in each issue. Then perhaps he has one or two essential pieces to fit in, features tied to the publication date or to recent news. After that, he looks to his stockpile. What will fit in? 'This one, that one and that. Fine – a nice mix.' He is content.

Now suppose that he has no stock of suitable material. He may then have to accept the best of the material that just happens to be submitted at that time. The alternative is to write something himself. Whatever he does, somehow he HAS to fill the pages. If his store is well-stocked he can be 'choosey'; if the cupboard is bare he will want to restock as soon as he can.

The purpose of the above description is not to invoke expressions of sympathy for the poor editor. It is to demonstrate the opportunities there are for you, for salesmanship.

As soon as you sell your first article to an editor, send him another one. Make sure that your second offer is every bit as good as that just accepted. If that one too is accepted, the editor will begin to recognize your name. Your work will be looked at favourably; the editor will hope that you are again offering him something he can use.

And one day, you may get a call from the editor asking you to write an article on a subject of his choice. An editorial commission!

Another hint follows from our description of the hard life of an editor. Keep your eyes open, and watch the reports in *Freelance Market News* etc., for news of new magazines. The editor of a new magazine will have no stockpile; he will usually be interested in developing new ideas; he will probably welcome writers with something new to offer.

But a word of warning. New magazines are sometimes short-lived. You may not get paid for published work if a magazine closes down (and even if you haven't been paid, once published, your First Rights will have gone – see later, Chapter 8). Your accepted but unused work in the stockpile may not be returned – but you'll naturally have kept a copy.

Never forget the importance of market study. If your work is what an editor wants, is *right* for his magazine, he'll buy it.

Hence the second golden rule of article-writing:

## KNOW YOUR MARKET

And know it well.

# 4

## THE ARTICLE CONTENT

You have your idea, you have done the subject research, and you have studied the market. Now you can start to think about the writing side of the business. (For the time being, we shall ignore the question of getting an editor's prior approval of the article idea. See Chapter 7.)

You are going to write an article: 'A short piece of non-fiction writing intended for sale.' (*The Concise Oxford Dictionary* defines an article as a 'literary composition [other than fiction] forming part of a magazine etc. but independent of others.' My definition is much the same, but shorter – and more realistic.) Consider that definition: an article is NOT the same as a school essay; it is NOT the same as an academic thesis; it is NOT the same as a technical report. The essential difference is that an article has to attract a purchaser. Put another way, an article has to *persuade* the reader to read it. If it is unlikely to interest – and therefore attract – the reader, no editor will buy it. And if it doesn't get bought, it doesn't get read.

The way to persuade a reader to get into your article is to grab him straight away. Then, once he is hooked, don't let him go until you finally round off the article at its end. We come on to those essential parts of an article – the start, the middle, and the end – later in this chapter. For now, consider how you are to handle the subject in the given space.

Your market study will have told you that the editor of your initial target magazine prefers 'your sort of article' to be perhaps eight hundred words long. Have you got an 800-word subject? In detail, this is something you can only learn from experience, but in general, the fitting of subject to length is not too difficult. You would not, I am sure, try to summarize the history of China in 800 words; that needs at least a book, and probably many books. But I have successfully related – in just 550 words – how one early Chinese emperor ordered a particular jade artefact made to aid him in his worship.

Clarify therefore, before starting to write, just what your article is to be about. Then confirm to yourself that you can do justice to that subject within the space available. It is no use offering even the most marvellous 2500-word article to an editor who never takes anything longer than 800 words.

A discipline often adopted by lecturers and other speakers is to define their objective before they start. This might be in such terms as: 'Having heard this lecture/talk, the listener should be able to print his own forged banknotes', or '... brew a cup of tea', or '... know how to prune his roses'. It is often worth applying a similar self-discipline to article-writing. It can help to ensure a consistency of approach throughout the article. It will certainly help to avoid the 'So what?' article – wherein an often unclear (if any) objective is not fulfilled; and the 'double-subject' article – which starts with one subject and then, changing horses in midstream, moves to another, ending up not satisfying the reader on either.

## Planning the article

Having mentally identified the purpose and carefully chosen the subject of your article, it is now possible to plan it in some datail. Start with a blank sheet of paper. At the top, write the subject and, where appropriate, the objective. The subject is not the article's eventual title, merely your working identification.

Next, working from the notes and papers that are the product of your research, list the facts and fancies that are to make up your article. The list, at this stage, will be in no particular order: it is just a list. Review the facts, etc. Have you enough to really fill an article of the length you plan? If not, can you get more? Whence?

Remember though, that an article cannot be merely an assembly of unsweetened facts. It is the job – almost the *raison d'etre* – of the article-writer to make the facts palatable. The reader must be interested. So perhaps you *do* have enough factual material after all. Perhaps what you lack is the jam filling that turns the stodgy doughnut into a sticky-fingered delight? Can you find some unusual, and therefore interesting, snippet of information, an apposite quote, or an amusing story, to leaven the factual lump?

Once you are content that you have enough material – or better, a little too much, so that you can pick and choose – you are ready to mould it into shape.

Here, I cannot help you much. Only you can decide on the shape or structure that you should adopt – the order in which you present the facts and fancies on offer. (And your market study may have suggested the structure that your target magazine is most likely to prefer.)

You can organize your article so that the facts follow each other in historical order. Or you can arrange them as a story, with historical flashbacks. 'How-to' articles are of course best structured in a sequential form. But other types of practical advice article are sometimes best structured with the most important advice first – or last. (In a 'How-to' article I wrote on simple photography for article-writers, I outlined several basic rules in what I considered to be their order of importance.)

If you are putting together the type of general interest article which is effectively a collection of random facts about a subject, try to open with a particularly strange and interesting fact – and finish with another. Start with a bang and go out the same way. And maintain the excitement at much the same level in the middle too.

Circularity is also a useful element in an article plan. In the final paragraph, refer back in some way to the start of the article. Make it clear to the reader that you've delivered what you 'promised'.

The most important thing about the structure of an article is that it be logical, that the facts fit together sensibly, that the case is proven. And all, of course, while retaining the reader's interest.

## Using a model

Just as budding artists learn their craft by copying the works of the great masters, so too can writers. Unfortunately though, few do. In essence, for the tiro writer it means – at least initially – modelling your work closely on similar published work. It does NOT mean copying a published article. Apart from the ethics, the subject will not sell twice in the same place. But working to an up-to-date model will help you to offer work of a style acceptable to the editor.

Find an article in a recent issue of your target magazine, of the length you propose to write and of a vaguely similar type. (A 'How-to' model for a 'How-to' copy; a personal experience model for a personal experience copy; a stately home visit model for a stately home visit copy; etc.) Pull that article to pieces. This is much the same process as the general market study, but in more detail.

Read the model article very carefully. Note the lightness, or otherwise, of the writer's tone. Note particularly the first paragraph: this is all that many people will ever read. Note the number of separate 'stories' that are included in the whole. (By 'story' I mean the section of text, often two or three paragraphs, which deals with a single aspect of the subject.) Count the total number of paragraphs in the article and the number per 'story'. Count the number of words in each sentence and in each paragraph: and this time, literally count every word. Look carefully too at the words themselves – how long, how 'difficult' are they?

I have seen it suggested that a good way of *getting into the feel* of a model article is to rewrite or retype it yourself, word for word. I haven't tried this, but I can see how it might help. (It's rather like preparing a brand-new typescript plus disk for a revised edition of a book – like this.)

You may think that I am obsessed with counting numbers of words. I have often been accused of this. But every successful writer counts words – I am perhaps just more thorough (finicky even) than others. (In his excellent book, *Writing a Novel* [Eyre Methuen, 1974], John Braine said, 'A writer is a person who writes, a writer is a person who counts words.' And the word count is far more crucial to a thousand-word article-writer than to an eighty-thousand-word novelist.) Initially at least, I commend my finicky/thorough approach to you. Unless you count every word, it is easy to miss the important yet subtle differences between styles.

*Study every word*

## An analysis example

I have analysed an article that was published, some while ago, in a typically brash, 'tabloidy' general interest magazine. The title is provocative, a good 'hook': 'Get 'em off – and get results' – but the content is really about successful ways of making a protest. The article is 580 words long in 22 paragraphs. The longest paragraph is 48 words long, the shortest is a 10-word single sentence. The average paragraph length is only 26 words. No paragraph contains more than four sentences – and many paragraphs are only one or two sentences long. Some sentences are quite long – one contains 34 words – but many are very short. The shortest sentence is only 6 words long, and the average overall is 15 words per sentence. I've counted – and studied – every word.

There are eight 'stories' in the article, each told in two or three short paragraphs. The 'stories are:

- thirty mothers breast-feeding their children in a crowded High Street shop – to demonstrate the lack of alternative facilities for this;
- a nude Italian girl asks for a bath at the mayor's house – the only house in the village still supplied with water;
- a man takes off his clothes in the social security office – to draw attention to his need for a clothes grant;
- the owner of a faulty chair sits on it, on top of his car, outside the shop he bought it from;
- a farmer returns rubbish dumped in his field to the garden of the 'dumper';
- artist dumps manure outside a newspaper office – for the use of their art critic;
- a housewife goes on strike and pickets her own house – until the family agree to help with the housework;
- a man complains to the council about the distractingly 'sexy noises' coming from the next-door bathroom.

Notice that the suggestive title only relates to three of the stories.

It would be pointless to offer the editor of that particular magazine another article about unusual methods of protesting for the next few years. But given an idea, and the knowledge, for a 500-

600 word article on another suitable subject – off the top of my head: about furnishing a house, perhaps, with the emphasis inevitably on the bedroom – your article could be modelled on the protest one.

For that specific target magazine you would need to write in sentences averaging about 15 words long; these sentences should build into paragraphs no more than 50 words long, averaging about half that length. (For more on sentence and paragraph lengths, see next chapter.) You'd need, say, six to nine 'stories' to fill out your article. The 'stories' wouldn't have to be as titillating as those in the protest piece – but with many magazines this would be a welcome bonus.

## Constituents of an article

Think now of what constitutes a magazine article. We have already defined it as 'short, saleable, non-fiction'. Its constituent parts each contribute to its saleability. They are:

- the title
- the opening paragraph
- the middle
- the closing paragraph

and perhaps

- the illustrations (see Chapter 6)

Each of these constituents has a role to play within the integrated whole. Each part is worth examining in detail.

## Titles

The title of an article is the first thing anyone notices. Sometimes, if you are lucky, it is featured on the front cover of the magazine;

usually it is mentioned on the Contents page; invariably it heads the article itself, in large bold print. It is the title that catches the roving eye of the 'flip-through' bookshop browser. A particularly good title may influence an editor's decision on your article. Certainly, a really good title will cause many an editor to pause in his sequence of rejections and glance at what's beneath it.

A title needs to have *impact*.

A long title often has all the dynamism of a large bowl of semolina pudding. The browser will give up half-way through. Ideally, try for a short, snappy title; one that will immediately capture the casual interest. But ... sometimes a long title can be gripping. There are no firm rules. As a general guide though, most people agree that shorter titles – say five words at most – are better than longer ones.

Ideas for titles are all around you: listen out for catchy, snappy, 'phrases-of-the-day'. (I gave one of my articles the title 'Write On' ... but it still didn't sell.) Study the titles of other published articles – a slight twist, together with a changed subject, might fit them admirably for yours. Consider too, the use of alliterative phrases: phrases made up of words with a common beginning letter have instant impact.

Think about titles whenever you have a spare moment – while waiting for the train, or for the five-o'clock whistle. Titles themselves often lead to article ideas: from time to time you will think of a marvellous title and then write an article to go with it.

(Some while ago, sitting on the top deck of a bus crawling snail-like around Parliament Square in London, I noted the statues of dissidents-of-their-time, Oliver Cromwell, Emmeline Pankhurst and – just around the corner – Boadicea. The perfect title came to me in a flash: 'Statues of Dissent'; the illustrated article soon followed – in fact, two different articles, a year apart, both using the same title.)

In my view, most titles fit into five broad categories. The categories as such are not important – but reviewing them can, of itself, often help you to come up with a good title. The categories, with examples, nearly all my own, are:

● the label – the simplest title of all and often the most effective;

*Examples*: 'Japanese Netsuke.' 'Jade – China's most precious stone.' 'The Witching Time.' (See also, Chapter 5.)

- the question – with which can be included, the often useful provocative statement;
  *Examples*: 'Are you the right type to be a "supersec"?' 'What's in a Name?' 'English men make better ...'
- the quotation – or sometimes better, the twisted quotation;
  *Examples*: 'To be or not to be, That is the question' (about achieving promotion). 'Lift up thine eyes' (about things to look out for, above eye level). 'Evil's the root of much money.'
- the exclamatory statement or 'screamer' – one of the few occasions when an article-writer may use an exclamation mark;
  *Examples*: 'Mayday!' (about 1 May). 'Here be Dragons!'
- the pun – and even a weak one will serve its purpose.
  *Examples*: 'The Write Approach.' 'Unfickle Jade.' 'Cashing in on history' (about old coins). 'Keep this under your Hat' (about all sorts of hats).

The editor will not always agree with your idea of a good title. As long as he buys your article, this is his prerogative. He may replace your sickly pun with a simple label. Or he may think up a more provocative title. It is always interesting – and often instructive – to observe such editorial 'improvements'. (Whatever you do though, don't be *prima-donna*-ish; don't complain, let him have his way.)

## Opening paragraphs – the hook

While the title of an article may be the lure, the bait that attracts the flip-through browser, the opening paragraph is the hook that catches him. The first paragraph is all that the casual reader will read – unless it grabs him, and his interest, very firmly. The first paragraph must be punchy; it is the 'taster'; it must go with a bang.

As with titles, I think it is helpful to categorise opening paragraphs into five basic types, somewhat similar to the title categories:

- the simple statement – the opening equivalent of the label title;
  *Example*: 'What gold is to the European, jade has always been to the Chinese. They value jade not only for its beauty, but also for its hardness and its seemingly endless life.'
- the question – usually provocative;
  *Example*: 'Are your pockets bulging, your handbags unclosable, and your drawers overbrimming – with certificates, statements and sales slips? Do you really need to keep all this paper? Or are you hoarding it unnecessarily?'
- the quotation – usually 'straight', for example, from a recent news item;
  *Example*: '"Ming umbrella-stand sells for £250,000." We have all seen such newspaper reports and looked wistfully at the favourite – but cracked – willow-pattern plate hanging on the kitchen wall.'
- the 'shocker' – the equivalent of the exclamatory or 'screamer' title;
  *Example*: 'In the time that it takes to ... <e.g., read this article>, ... <e.g., a thousand ... babies will be born.>'
- the anecdote – the story approach.
  *Example*: 'The editorial specification said 750 words plus illustrations. "Fine," said I. "That'll be easy." Although I knew the subject well, I still scribbled out the points I wanted to make.'

It is not necessary to use an opening paragraph of the same basic type as the title. Sometimes it works, sometimes it doesn't. And the market for which you are writing will influence your choice of opening. The more brash or lively the magazine, the more they will welcome flamboyant openings.

Remembering that the prime purpose of the opening paragraph is to hook and land the not-yet-interested reader, there are two qualities to aim at in writing it. The opening should seek to involve – to draw in – the reader; use the word 'you' whenever possible, and relevant. And the opening should ideally tell the reader something new and interesting – or make it obvious that what follows will be of interest.

The opening paragraph should be short. Short paragraphs are more punchy than long ones; they get to the point quicker; they are easier to read. The flip-through browser will seldom bother to 'taste' a long opening paragraph at all. As a rule of thumb, try making the first paragraph about half the average length. (If your article has an average paragraph length of fifty words, write your opening para about twenty-five to thirty words long.)

## Middle paragraphs – the meat

The reader's attention firmly seized by the opening paragraph, it is now up to you to hold that interest throughout the article. You must 'play the reader along' until he gets to the end.

The body of your article should be full of interesting information – but it must not read like a catalogue of facts, or an extract from an encyclopedia. Interesting information can be provided not only in the form of facts and statistics, but also wrapped up in anecdotes and quotes.

We have already discussed, in Chapter 2, the sources of the material that will go into the body of the article. And we have noticed how, in our model article, the facts are assembled in a number of 'stories'. It is part of the craft of the article-writer to present the facts and statistics in an interesting way.

Statistics and numerical facts are important – but potentially dull. The writer can add a little sparkle, a little interest, to them by making comparisons. When I lived in what is now the Malaysian State of Sabah, I wrote about it, of course. Seldom though did I say simply that Sabah covered just over 29,000 square miles; such areal statistics mean little to most readers. It was always better, after mentioning the size, to illustrate it by explaining that it was more than three times the size of Wales ... or just over a tenth of the size of Texas. (The choice of such comparisons will naturally depend on the market you are targeting.) It is usually best to give readers the actual statistics as well as illustrating them by comparison. Avoid particularly describing the size of something merely as 'very' – very big, very small, etc. Quantify: say how big, how small. (Indeed, I try to avoid using the word 'very' almost anywhere. It is almost always either an imprecise or an unnecessary – as in 'very unique' – qualifier.)

Anecdotes too are important: and good anecdotes are never dull.

But you may not have been able to collect enough anecdotal material, as recommended in Chapter 2. In such a situation there is nothing wrong in producing your own anecdote. An anecdote is no more than a fact or an experience expressed in story form. So long as your facts or experiences are accurate, they can often be retold in a more useful form. Try not to do it too often though – made-up anecdotes can lack the freshness of reality.

I knew that pieces of jade were being sold cheaply in a nearby town. I had bought some; that was a fact. I needed a female-oriented anecdote to fit an article in progress. So I invented a fictional housewife who went gift shopping, reporting her conversation with the dealer from whom she bought some cheap jade pieces.

The gist of the conversation was real: it was actually between the dealer and I – a male person. Here was no invention of facts, merely a 'fictionalization' of them. Within the limits of probability, this is perfectly acceptable.

And don't forget that the ideal anecdotes are often those relating your own mishaps. You are the ideal person to appear in your articles as 'the stooge', the 'fall-guy'. You, best of all, can show how to avoid the same mishap recurring; the reader will identify with you. (Notice how I am using my own experiences in this book to illustrate potential problems, faults, etc.)

Quotations too, like anecdotes, help to make an article come alive. By their nature they represent the views of other people – people with whom the reader can perhaps identify. They add the weight of someone else's views – someone perhaps well-known – to the comments of the unknown article-writer.

Do not assume that all views and opinions quoted in an article were collected at first hand by the writer. Quotations used in articles can indeed come from personal interviews, but some come from other sources. You can quote from interviews published elsewhere; you can quote from a source's published articles and books; or, always useful, from published books of quotations. In books of quotations the hard work has been done for you; the nuggets of wit and wisdom have been sorted out by subject. (But keep all quotations short – say fifty words at most – to avoid copyright infringement.)

Looking in one of my own several books of quotations, I find, for instance, that George Bernard Shaw – of course – made a tyically witty and relevant comment. He said, 'I often quote myself. It adds spice to my conversation.' When you are as well known, you can try this – until then, quote others. All fitting quotations add spice.

## Closing paragraphs

When you come to the end of your article, you need to round it off conclusively. There is nothing worse, in an article, than just ... stopping. That merely looks as though you are exhausted – devoid of further facts or sufficient ability; that must never be so. Ideally, you need another startling fact, another 'bang', on a par with the opening paragraph, to end on. If you have used the best of your available material in the opening paragraph, try to save the next-best item for the end.

If you haven't got anything spectacular with which to end, then try for some other way of rounding off the package. Bring the reader back to the purpose of the article; remind him how, having read the article, he can now better cope with something. Or try for a mildly witty conclusion. (I ended a solid factual article about the need to keep paper – bills, statements, etc. – by disclaiming any ability to advise on how to keep paper money. That, I left to the reader.)

And because, in its own way, the closing paragraph is as important as the opening, strive again for *impact*. Keep the length of the final paragraph as short as the opener too. This will help.

## Writing methods

Finally, because everyone is always interested in the unimportant personal details, how – physically – should you write? This has to be a matter of personal choice. I can only tell you what I did when I was a 'spare-time' writer, early on, and what I do now.

Nowadays I work on a word processor – and more about that below.

Before I had that though, I used to write all of my articles in longhand, on alternative lines of narrow-lined A4 hole-punched paper. (One advantage of such paper is that it is commonly used by impoverished students; the chain stationers therefore usually sell 'Jumbo' pads cheaply – on 'Special Offer' – in the late summer, just before term starts.

Writing on alternate lines left enough space for the many changes I made to the first draft. My writing was, and is, often tiny. Figure 4.1 reproduces a page of my handwritten drafting – and shows how I change words, phrases, etc. as I go along. The alternate lines and tiny writing allowed me to partly polish my work (see Chapter 5) without rewriting whole pages. I then typed what was hopefully the final version, completing the revising/polishing process as I translated my tiny scribbles and corrections into typescript.

At first, I often found the need to correct, or further improve my initial typescript. But retyping takes time. You soon learn to make all your major changes on the handwritten pages leaving only the most minor polishing improvements to be made while typing.

Irrespective of the many advantages of a word processor, it is still perfectly practical to work this way. Indeed, many established writers, set in their ways, continue to draft in longhand before final typing. The only essential is that the end result be in typescript. (And few of us can afford to pay someone else to type for us.)

If you are just starting and haven't yet got a word processor, I commend to you the method outlined above. It worked – for years – for me; it will work for you.

But today, as I've said, I write directly on my word processor.

As I type them, the words appear on the monitor screen in front of me. And I can easily change them – again and again, until I think I've got it right. (The previous two sentences were altered immediately I had written them. At first, I had started with 'The words appear on ...' but suddenly realized that the sentence would flow better if I started with 'As I type them, the words ...' The next sentence started off as 'And I can alter them ...' which again was instantly amended to 'And I can easily change them ...')

The word processor lets me work directly into typescript while at the same time affording me exactly the same facility as my

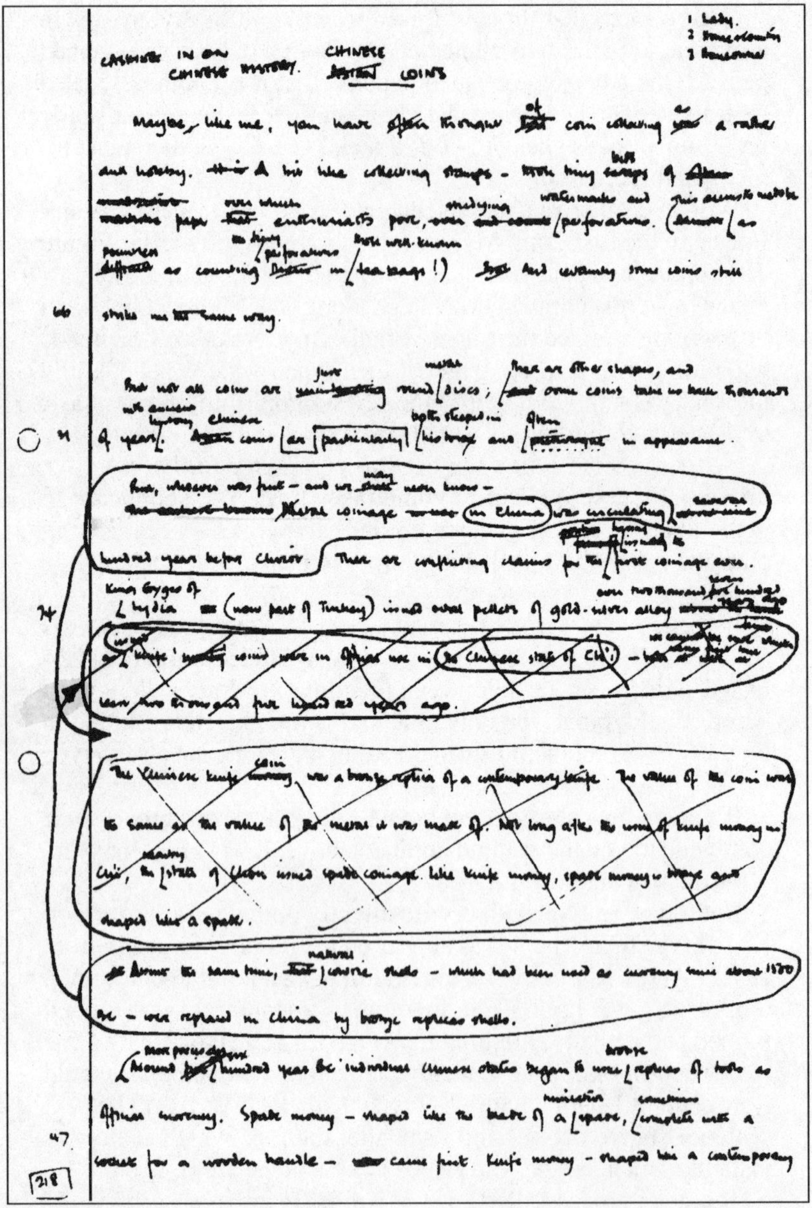
CASHING IN ON CHINESE HISTORY. CHINESE COINS

Maybe, like me, you have thought of coin collecting as a rather arid hobby. A bit like collecting stamps – little tiny scraps of paper over which enthusiasts pore, studying watermarks and perforations. (As pointless as counting the tiny perforations on tea-bags!) And certainly some coins still strike me that way.

But not all coins are just round metal discs; there are other shapes, and some coins take us back thousands of years. Chinese coins are particularly historic and often both shaped in history in appearance.

Who was first – and we may never know – metal coinage was circulating in China several hundred years before Christ. There are conflicting claims for the first coinage ever. King Gyges of Lydia (now part of Turkey) issued oval pellets of gold-silver alloy over two thousand five hundred years ago.

Around the same time, natural cowrie shells – which had been used as currency since about 1500 BC – were replaced in China by bronze replica shells.

Around hundred years BC individual Chinese states began to issue bronze replicas of tools as official currency. Spade money – shaped like the blade of a miniature spade, sometimes complete with a socket for a wooden handle – came first. Knife money – shaped like a contemporary

Figure 4.1 A typical page from one of my earlier hand-written draft manuscripts – before I had a word processor. Drafting by hand is a practical approach for the beginner: word processors merely make life easier.

handwriting method to change my words again and again. The word processor lets me type fast – much faster than I ever achieved on a typewriter (but less accurately) – with the added bonus of being able to correct at leisure. I can refine and polish as many times as I like. The problem is now one of knowing when to stop and say, 'That's as good as I'm going to get it.'

One further bonus of the word processor: I retain electronic copies of all my articles (and now my books, too) and can print out a fresh copy at any time. Or extract and re-use a particular description. I include a little more advice – 'a little' only because it is almost impossible to keep up-to-date with matters computing – on word processors in Chapter 7.

As to *when* I write, I don't think this matters; the important thing – the third golden rule – is that you should:

## WRITE OFTEN AND REGULARLY

If you don't write often and regularly, your 'writing muscle' will grow slack. You need to keep in trim.

Whilst I was a wage-slave, I wrote for about an hour each evening, after dinner. I also spent several hours at my desk each weekend. Keeping to that routine I wrote – and sold – hundreds of articles and several books.

For several years now, I have been a full-time writer. No longer having to commute to a London office, I am at my desk by about 9 most days and work fairly steadily until 5 or 6 – with a commensurate output. Inevitably though, the 'work' is far more than just writing; there is much correspondence ... and many administrative chores.

# 5

# STRINGING THE WORDS TOGETHER

The task of the writer is to communicate. Unless he conveys his mesage to the reader, his writing is all a waste of time. The writer communicates with words: words strung together in sentences, building into paragraphs and linking together to form the whole. Words make sentences make paragraphs make articles.

Each and every word must be chosen with care. Each word must be a 'communicating' word – not one chosen to impress the reader. Unless you communicate, you will not sell. Editors buy 'interest' – not 'cleverness'.

Writing – the sort that will sell – is hard work. If anyone tells you that he just sits down and the words flow easily, he is either an unpublished writer ... or a born genius. (And there's not many of them around.) When you are writing for sale you must at all times ponder on whether the typical reader will understand. And not just understand – for there are no 'captive readers' – but be really interested by and enjoy your writing. Even if the reader understands, but is not gripped, he will often not bother to read. That's another reason why every word you use must be chosen with great (and tender loving) care.

## Style

There are few, if any, fixed rules about writing. And were I to be so rash as to propound one, someone is certain to break it – successfully. Even much of the grammar that used to be taught at school is no longer so important as it once was. Note for instance how frequently writers – not just me – and politicians too, start sentences with 'And' or 'But'.

And how often do we see a well-split infinitive? (Some editors correct my split infinitives – most no longer bother. We are all more inclined *to boldly go* ...)

The nearest thing to rules on how to write that I can offer is the writer's ABC. Let your writing be:

A  Accurate – which is a matter of careful research. If you make a mistake, someone is sure to notice it and write to the editor. If that happens often (at all?) your credibility will wane, and with it, your sales.

B  Brief – concise might be a better word, or 'don't waste words'.

C  Clear – and simple. Use 'easy' words in easily-read sentences.

Leaving aside the matter of accuracy, the research base for which was investigated in Chapter 2, the two remaining qualities are brevity and clarity. And these two qualities go neatly together. Concise writing is usually clear.

This chapter opened with the concept that words make sentences make paragraphs make articles. Everything starts with the words – so shall we. It is obvious, if you stop to think about it, that your reader will probably find it hard to understand any word that you yourself had to seek out in the dictionary or Thesaurus. The average reader will not enjoy struggling over difficult words. And he will automatically classify all long, unusual words as 'difficult'.

Try not to use words in your article-writing that you would not use in everyday speech; if you must use the dictionary or Thesaurus, seek out the best-known, the shortest and easiest alternative on offer. It comes back to communicating rather than seeking to impress the reader with your literary skill. A useful rule of thumb is to stop and think hard before using any word of three or more syllables. (In this test, ignore those relatively simple words made long by the use of endings such as *-ed*, *-ment*, or *-ly*; and any words which are the result of joining two simple words together.)

Mark Twain expressed his preference for short simple words in a delightfully business-like way: 'I never write *metropolis* for seven cents, when I can get the same price for *city*.'

But don't carry too far the search for short simple words. If the RIGHT word is a long one, use it. Then explain its meaning.

## Counting words

As the words build up into sentences, keep these short too. There is nothing wrong with a long sentence, except that it is hard to write well. It is all too easy to get carried away with balancing clause and counter-clause; and the 'beauty of the well-turned phrase'. It is also easy to omit the verb – or put in one too many.

A short sentence is easier to write – and write well. All you need is a subject, an object and a verb. If a short sentence is easier to write, why struggle trying to write a long one?

Short sentences are also easier to understand. An American study showed that when sentence lengths reach more than about 25 words, only 10 per cent of readers can understand them. (I only just got that thought into a maximum length sentence. But remember: these are mere guides, not rules carved on stone tablets.) Unless I am working to a model with even shorter lengths, I usually write to an average sentence length of about 15 words – and a maximum of 25. Occasionally I go over that top limit. (But I do it consciously.) And note that I suggest working to a much shorter average. With a maximum of 25 and an average of 15, there have to be some extremely short – 5-word – sentences too.

Don't let this sentence-length guidance lead you to write all near-average-length sentences. Vary your sentence-lengths around the average. An article consisting of all 15-word sentences would be a dull – even if easy – read. All 25-word sentences would, at best, lull the reader to sleep; a string of 5-word sentences would create an exciting breathless atmosphere (fine in a thriller perhaps). For articles, write some long sentences, some short, and some middling-length.

When counting words in sentences, treat a colon or semi-colon – conventionally the end-punctuation of a self-contained clause – as the equivalent of a full-stop. But in most articles, full-stops and commas alone are the best punctuation.

A useful discipline is to think out the whole of each sentence before you write it down. Of itself, this approach will usually lead to shorter, simpler sentences. Who – other than perhaps a new Jane Austen – could hold a complex 60-word sentence in their mind without putting pen to paper? Another useful idea is, once it's written down, to read your work aloud. This ensures that you don't write anything you would have difficulty in getting your tongue around.

An American management writing guru, Robert Gunning, expresses this readability concept as the advice, 'Write like you talk'. This may be ungrammatical but it is helpfully explicit. And it fits in well with the advice of author Don Marquis, who said: 'If you want to get rich from writing, write the sort of thing that's read by persons who move their lips when they're reading to themselves.'

Paragraphs too should be concise. Not necessarily short, but as short as they can sensibly be constructed.

Ideally, a paragraph deals with a single aspect of a subject; a single thought plus associated explanation. Sir Ernest Gower puts this well when he says that 'every paragraph must be homogeneous in subject matter'. He further explains that while an over-long homogeneous paragraph may be sub-divided, it is wrong to combine two or more short paragraphs into a longer paragraph of several thoughts.

## Good-looking paragraphs

The reason for advocating shorter words and sentences is to make them clearer and easier to read. Shorter paragraphs contribute less to the cause of easy reading. Rather, they are a matter of presentation. Look at any old book on your shelves – and some present-day 'academic' ones – or visualize an ancient newspaper. With long paragraphs the printed page was one solid block of grey. Breaks between paragraphs relieve the greyness. Shorter paragraphs increase the number of gaps in between: they increase the white space (at starting indents and finishing line-ends). They make the pages LOOK more attractive – and apparently easier to read.

As a further rule of thumb, when writing articles, I generally aim at an average paragraph length of about fifty to sixty words. And I usually work to a top limit of about eighty words.

(Books are different: paragraphs can be a little longer. The column width is greater in a book than in a magazine; this means less depth of type for the same length of paragraph. In books I aim at an eighty-word average and sometimes stretch as far as a hundred-and-fifty for the maximum.)

Do not, though, write all of your paragraphs the same length. That's boring. Vary their lengths, to impart an extra interest, a fluctuating rhythm, to your writing. Even use the occasional single short-sentence paragraph; these give a sudden *punch* to your writing.

Ideally, each first sentence should state the main thought contained in a paragraph. Subsequent sentences then develop and expand on that initial theme. The last sentence then rounds off that paragraph's thought. And because short sentences have greater impact than longer ones, there is much to be said for making first – and last – sentences short. But of course, to adjust sentence lengths slavishly and deliberately can easily spoil the natural flow of your writing. All I suggest is that you bear these thoughts in mind.

And keep words, sentences and paragraphs short.

The flow of your writing will be improved if you link consecutive paragraphs together – not physically, that's wrong, but in thought. These links can be achieved by starting a new paragraph with a passing reference to its predecessor. This will not always be possible, but where it is, paragraph linking makes the reading more easy.

Useful linking phrases with which paragraphs can begin include:

- 'But these are not isolated cases ...'
- 'Yet if you look around ...'
- 'Not only does ...'
- 'But that may never happen.'
- 'And ...'

## Punctuation

So far, we have ignored the matter of punctuation. But this is no longer the difficult matter that it might once have been. Short sentences seldom need more than a full stop. No problem there. Nor is there any great problem in adding the occasional comma to a slightly longer sentence: so long as it is only occasional. It is only in the really long sentences – which I recommend you eschew – that other punctuation marks are needed.

Avoid using the exclamation mark. Other than very rare use of it is the mark of an amateur. Your words should serve the same purpose. The question mark is easy to use. It is the mark of a question. The only 'difficult' punctuation marks are the colon and the semi-colon.

The colon is almost a full stop: it is a means of linking two short, separate, but associated thoughts. It is also the introduction – without a dash – to a list. Other than in listing it is best avoided unless you're totally confident with its use.

The semi-colon is half-way between a comma and a full stop; each related phrase separated by a semi-colon should be as complete as a sentence; a semi-colon should always be capable of being replaced by a full stop. Use the semi-colon with great care – or not at all.

You may have noticed that I use a lot of dashes, usually in pairs; publishers' copy-editors regard the dash as a lazy person's punctuation and often replace it; I prefer to think that it makes an article look more casual and relaxed – easier to read. Magazine editors are much more willing to accept the dashes in my writing. I recommend restraint in the use of dashes. But don't give 'em up; they're useful.

For the last page or two I have been advocating stylistic rules of thumb for article-writers. I commend these to beginning article-writers – but as you learn your trade, bend them to fit your own style. Ignore them if you wish. What is really important is that you write magazine articles – not essays, school compositions or academic theses. Articles sell: essays don't.

So ... the fourth golden rule:

## WRITE SIMPLY

## Checking up

In the previous section I have already stressed the importance of short sentences and paragraphs. To keep a check on the lengths and on the balance of one sentence or paragraph with another, it is necessary to count words.

As a beginner, until you acquire a *feel* for sentence and paragraph lengths, I recommend actually counting every word. For many many years – until I acquired my word processor – I counted every word that I wrote. And this practice took me through dozens and dozens of articles and more than a dozen books.

Count word by word, sentence by sentence, paragraph by paragraph every time you reach the foot of a page of double-spaced handwritten manuscript – about every 250-300 words. As you count, make a note of each sentence length: if two sentences within the same paragraph each exceed twenty words, think about the possible need to change one of them.

Today, I have a good *feel* for the number of words in a typed paragraph on screen; I still though, occasionally, check on the length of a sentence that looks long – and usually cut it.

While counting the words on each page, think about the writing in general, the comparative lengths, and the overall rhythm. Ask yourself:

- Are there many long words – or any 'over-long' ones? Can you explain anything more simply?
- Have you inadvertently slipped into the use of jargon that your reader will not understand?
- Does that paragraph consist of all long sentences? If so, can you perhaps add in one short one, to leaven the pill?
- Even though no sentence is 'too long', how is the average? Are they all much the same length? Vary them.
- Have you made the most important point in the first sentence of each paragraph – or have you buried it?
- Are the paragraph lengths too similar? Are they all too short, or – more often – too long?
- How is the overall length going – compared with the model to which you are working, and the material still to be incorporated?

It is sensible to correct all such faults before moving on to the next page of drafting. I recommend going through this checking process whether you are writing by hand or on a machine – and a page seems about the right amount of writing to be viewed as an entity. You are still only taking off the rough edges of your writing. The real *polishing* comes later.

Before the polishing though, let's finish the first draft; let's get to the end of your article.

Now check on the overall length. If it's too short – you must bring in more material. But it's more likely to be too long: longer than your model; longer than the subject deserves. This is no bad thing. It allows you room to *polish* your writing.


## Polishing

Everybody's work needs polishing – beginners and established authors alike. There is little writing that cannot be 'tightened up'; there are few writers whose work is not occasionally unclear; there is always a possibility that an imprecise word has slipped in. To weed out all the 'less-than-good' writing, you must review your work. (Refer back to Figure 4.1 for a partial example of how I polish.)

Read your whole article through again, *aloud.* (You want the words to come back to you through your ears, rather than reverberate silently inside your head.) This process will identify the phrases that you thought looked good on paper but which cannot easily be spoken aloud. It should also identify the long words and the jargon which you may use without thinking, but that others may find unusual.

Whilst reading the article aloud to yourself, watch out also for sudden warm flushes of literary pride. If you feel particularly pleased with the way you have worded a section of your article, of its sheer literary merit (and your skill) ... cross it out and rewrite it. Such feelings of pride almost certainly mean that it is not *simple* enough – and that must always be your aim. (If you yearn to display literary skill, try writing poetry, or long philosophical essays: but don't waste anyone's time trying to sell them.)

Having read your article aloud, and made your written work more akin to everyday spoken English, look again. This time read silently.

Reconsider every word. Is it necessary, or is it 'padding'? Ruthlessly cut out all padding. Is there an 'interesting' word that you found in the thesaurus or the dictionary? If so, try to find a more everyday word: if you had to look it up to make sure of the meaning, your reader may well not understand it. And he won't bother to look it up. Consider too whether you have qualified the unqualifiable. Examples such as *very* unique, *slightly* pregnant and *absolutely* dead demonstrate this often overlooked fault.

(Review each use of the word *very*. It is (very) seldom necessary. Think too about the word *and* used in mid-sentence; a full stop will often be better.)

Another common form of padding is the unnecessary sentence lead-in: 'I think that ...'; 'In order to ...'; 'And, of course, ...' Such phrases are little more than a written 'er – um – er' pause. They don't carry the reader forward at all; they are redundant, and they should be struck out.

Check your words to make sure that you have the meaning – and the spelling – correct. Time and again, when writing, I find that a word I propose to use does not mean exactly what I thought it did. This is usually when I am going for a longer word than I would use in speech: in other words, when I am breaking my own 'rules'. Time and again too I find that my spelling needs to be checked. Yours will too – no matter how competent you are sure you are. Use your dictionary often.

Should you need to emphasize points in your writing, do this by your choice of words and the structure of your sentences. Underlining is usually the hallmark of an amateur writer. And a technical point: underlined typescript – if left thus by the editor – will appear in print in *italics*. Italics don't look particularly emphatic: they should be reserved for foreign or unusual words (or for words used unusually), and for book and magazine titles.

Working through your manuscript, 'polishing out' the difficult phrases and the unnecessary words, you may decide that you need to rewrite the whole article.

Don't despair. For a beginner this is no bad thing. The rewrite will be much improved, much 'tighter'. Even for a more practised writer it is still not unusual – certainly I rewrite many individual paragraphs. And my post-polishing drafts are a maze of alterations, insertions and deletions, and of moved paragraphs.

When you have revised, rewritten and polished your work until you are satisfied with it, read it through aloud once again. Does it still sound natural, or have you polished away all the liveliness – all of your style? If so – rewrite it. And finally, count the words yet again. Is the overall length now/still about right? (It needs to be within about fifty words of your model for an article of a thousand words or less.)

## A worked example – 'Hallowe'en'

Let us look now at how I wrote the article on Hallowe'en that appears as Figure 5.1.

Some while ago, I had approached the editor of *Townswoman* – which at that time welcomed freelance contributions – seeking to purchase sample copies of the magazine. When writing, I said that I was thinking of offering her several articles, which I mentioned briefly. One suggestion, a commemorative feature on the socialist suffragette Sylvia Pankhurst, caught her eye; she asked for it urgently. I provided just what she wanted, quickly and in time. My professionalism paid off: a few weeks later the editor telephoned me, out of the blue.

'I want six hundred words about Hallowe'en,' she said. 'Tell the readers what it is, how it came into being – all that sort of thing.'

'But I don't know anything about Hallowe'en,' I protested.

'Then you'll enjoy doing the research, won't you?' was the cheerful response. 'I want the copy by ...'

Clearly I couldn't escape – not that I wanted to – so I had me a commission. I have had a few other wholly unprompted commissions in my time, but they don't come so frequently that they can be passed up. And the editor was right; I did enjoy finding out. I really didn't know anything about the subject – everything in the article was new to me.

I collected the material from various books on my own shelves, from a couple of books found for me by my friendly local

# The witching time

**It's Hallowe'en time again and Gordon Wells tells us about its pagan origins**

DESPITE ITS present emphasis on children demanding a hand-out with 'trick-or-treat' threats of mischief, Hallowe'en is not an original American custom. Even the pumpkin lantern faces are of Irish origin — a development of their 'jack-o'-lanterns'. Like many other Christian festivals, Hallowe'en — All Hallows Eve, the eve of All Saints' Day — has its origins in Celtic paganism.

The Celtic year was based on the farming calendar. The year began on November 1: the start of winter; the end of the growing and harvesting time; the time for mating the sheep and slaughtering livestock surpluses for winter food. The turn of the year was celebrated in the great festival of Samain (or Samhain), the Lord of the Dead. The other great Celtic festival was that of Beltine (or Beltane), held on May 1 to celebrate the end of winter. The festival of Samain was a solemn, often frightening occasion; that of Beltine was a time of rejoicing. The eve of Samain, the end of the old year, was thought to be a between time — belonging neither to the old year nor to the new. It was the night when time stood still. Then, neither time nor the boundary of the nether world was well defined. The 'natural' laws were in suspension and demons, ghosts and witches wandered at will. It was a night when wise men stayed home and locked their doors.

One feature of the festival of Samain was the lighting of bonfires. These were intended to help the sun survive through the long winter. Meanwhile, they also served to protect the people from the denizens of the nether world. The bonfires of course survived, not just at Hallowe'en but now, more commonly, a few days later in commemoration of the infamous activist Guy Fawkes. But Hallowe'en fires themselves continued to burn, on burial mounds and hill-tops, right through until the latter part of the last century. At Fortingall in Scotland, an annual bonfire was lit on an ancient burial mound until 1924 — when the custom was finally stopped because it interfered with the grouse.

All Saints' Day — to honour those saints without their own special day — was originally established in the seventh century as a May festival. But the awesome festival of Samain was still celebrated with too much pagan enthusiasm to be long ignored by the Christian church. In the eighth century All Saints' Day was transferred from May to November. Samain became Hallowe'en.

Hallowe'en remained a night of mystic fear throughout the Middle Ages.

### Grotesque changes

Around the end of the 17th century, the festival of Hallowe'en began to change. Villages now donned grotesque masks and represented themselves as ghosts and demons. They went from house to house, singing, dancing, and collecting offerings of appeasement originally left for the real ghosts. These masked 'guisers', as they were called, then led the unseen evil spirits off to the outskirts of town and away. It was then only a short step — of a century or so — to involve the children, with costumes and door-to-door collections. By the beginning of the present century, Hallowe'en was largely dying out in England. (The irish and the Scots continued to celebrate it.) The English Hallowe'en was largely absorbed into the Bonfire Night celebrations.

Hallowe'en flourished in America after it was taken there in the 1840s and their 'trick-or-treat' customs were developed. Brought back by US servicemen in the 1939-45 war, the American way of Hallowe'en has since been regaining popularity in England. Few houses today are safe from occasional 'trick-or-treat' visitations.

The Lord Samain would no doubt turn in his grave. If only time would once again stand still, for just one night — or perhaps it does?

Figure 5.1 A worked example: an article of mine about Hallowe'en, as published in *The Townswoman*.

librarian – and from asking everyone within earshot what they could tell me. I had none of my usually preferred batches of newspaper cuttings to fall back on. But research techniques are not what we are looking at in this chapter. We are considering how to write.

My submitted article was entitled 'Hallowe'en – the night when time stands still'. But the editor changed that, as you can see. (I thought my title was quite good – if rather long – but the payment cheque amply compensated me for its disappearance.)

The opening paragraph of my submission was:

> For all its present emphasis on demanding a hand-out with 'Trick-or-Treat' threats of mischief, Hallowe'en is not an
> 24   original American custom. Even the pumpkin lantern-faces are
> 15   of Irish origin – a development of their 'Jack-o'-lanterns'.

(The figures at the left margin are the number of words in the sentence ending on that line.)

I had wondered how to start the article off and decided to take a well-known feature of Hallowe'en – a possibly unpopular one with *Townswoman* readers too – and debunk it. It is partly a 'simple statement' opener and partly a 'shocker' – to use the categories listed in the previous chapter (page 56/7). The opening sentence was rather longer than I would have liked, but it worked well. The only editorial changes were to substitute 'Despite' for 'For all', and to take out the capitals I had used in 'Trick-or-Treat'. (I had been inconsistent.)

My second paragraph – short and, I thought, mildly provocative to a possibly conservative readership – was run into the first when it got into print. (To my mind, running the two paragraphs together reduced the 'separated' emphasis that I was seeking with the second paragraph.)

> Like many other Christian festivals, Hallowe'en – All Hallows Eve, the eve of All Saints' Day – has its origins in Celtic
> 21   paganism.

Being part of the refutation of the American origins, this amalgamation was perfectly sensible editing. Both of my paragraphs were part of 'the same thought'. And the editor explained to me later that she couldn't really spare *the space* for short paragraphs. (Remember the reason why I advocated them?)

Note that in my first two paragraphs I used a total of 60 words in three sentences: an average of 20 words per sentence. I brought my average down in the next few paragraphs.

The next three paragraphs in my submission were all about the Celtic festivals and the Celtic calendar. Again, more or less the same 'story' or thought, so it was not unreasonable that the editor ran the three together. (In my original, handwritten draft, I had myself written the first two as one, decided it was too long, and split it into two.)

| | |
|---|---|
| 9 | The Celtic year was based on the farming calendar. The year |
| 5,4 | began on November 1: the start of winter; the end of the growing |
| 8 | and harvesting time; the time for mating the sheep, and |
| 13 | slaughtering livestock surpluses for winter food. The turn of the |
| | year was celebrated in the great festival of Samain (or Samhain), |
| 20 | the Lord of the Dead. |

Notice here how the first brief sentence makes the main point, elaborated in susequent sentences. Note too the use of punctuation in the second sentence. 'The year began on November 1:' introduces several elaborations – a list – explaining that statement. Each explanatory phrase ends with a semi-colon. And the whole construction effectively produces a lot of short 'sentence-equivalents', thereby reducing the average sentence length (to under 14 words) and making the paragraph easier to understand. Each colon and semi-colon could, at a pinch, have been replaced by a full-stop.

The next two of 'my' paragraphs are part of the same general thought. They again express the main thought in each first sentence and help to keep the average sentence-length down.

| | |
|---|---|
| | The other great Celtic festival was that of Beltine (or Beltane), |
| 22 | held on May 1 to celebrate the end of winter. The festival of |
| 10 | Samain was a solemn, often frightening, occasion; that of |
| 8 | Beltine was a time of rejoicing. |

| | |
|---|---|
| | The eve of Samain, the end of the old year, was thought to be a |
| | 'between' time – belonging neither to the old year nor to the |
| 27,8 | new. It was the night when time stood still. Then, neither time |

13    nor the boundary of the nether world was well defined. The
      'natural' laws were in suspension and demons, ghosts and
14    witches wandered at will. It was a night when wise men stayed
13    home and locked their doors.

In the second of the above paragraphs, notice how, while the main point is made in the rather long first sentence (and the dash might here be thought of as a semi-colon-equivalent), the second sentence carries emphasis – largely by its short sharp message, 'It was the night when time stood still.' Within these two paragraphs the average sentence length is only fourteen words – and not one word is a long one.

My next two paragraphs dealt with Hallowe'en bonfires: I had separated them because of the time difference; the editor once again ran them together because of their content.

12    One feature of the festival of Samain was the lighting of bonfires.
      These were intended to help the sun to survive through the long
13    winter. Meanwhile, they also served to protect the people from
15    the denizens of the nether world. The bonfires of course
      survived, not just at Hallowe'en but now more commonly, a few
      days later, in commemoration of the infamous activist Guy
25    Fawkes.

      But Hallowe'en fires themselves continued to burn, on burial
      mounds and hill-tops, right through until the latter part of the
22    last century. At Fortingall in Scotland, an annual bonfire was lit
16    on an ancient burial mound until 1924 – when the custom was
12    finally stopped because it interfered with the grouse.

Notice how I linked the two original paragraphs by the 'But Hallowe'en fires themselves continued to burn ...' I then followed that up with the nearest thing to an anecdote that I could manage. (It was also a veiled social comment: the popular old custom had to give way to the sport of the gentry.)

I was a little worried about using the word 'denizens' in the first of these two paragraphs. It is not a word in day-to-day use – but I decided that the readers of *Townswoman* were unlikely to find it difficult or distracting. I would probably not have used it in an article for *My Weekly*.

My next paragraph (below) dealt with the religious takeover of the Celtic festival. Although relatively short by the editor's standards, it stood alone. And the next paragraph too, even though extremely short, needed to stand alone to give the impact that I sought. The editor agreed with my judgement.

|    | |
|----|-|
|    | All Saint's Day – to honour those saints without their own |
|    | special day – was originally established in the seventh century |
| 23 | as a May festival. But the awesome festival of Samain was still |
|    | celebrated with too much pagan enthusiasm to be long ignored |
| 22 | by the Christian chruch. In the eighth century All Saints' Day |
| 13 | was transferred from May to October. Samain became |
| 3  | Hallowe'en. |

|    | |
|----|-|
|    | Hallowe'en remained a night of mystic fear throughout the |
| 11 | Middle Ages. |

Notice particularly that final sentence in the first of the above paragraphs. Its very shortness gives it urgency and impact: *Samain became Hallowe'en*. No ifs, no buts: just a bald statement of fact. And the three-word sentence balances the three longer sentences that preceded it. The average sentence length in that paragaph is only 15 despite two sentences each containing twenty-plus words.

We now come more up to date – which is acknowledged by the editor in her sub-heading. Again, she ran my next two paragraphs together. Both deal with the changes in European customs, so the running together was not unreasonable.

|    | |
|----|-|
|    | Around the end of the seventeenth century, the festival of |
| 14 | Hallowe'en began to change. Villagers now donned grotesque |
| 12 | masks and represented themselves as ghosts and demons. They |
|    | went from house to house, singing, dancing, and collecting |
| 19 | offerings of appeasement originally left for the real ghosts. These |
|    | masked 'guisers', as they were called, then led the unseen evil |
| 21 | spirits off to the outskirts of town and away. |

|    | |
|----|-|
|    | It was then only a short step – of a century or so – to involve |
| 23 | the children, with costumes and door-to-door collections. By the |
|    | beginning of the present century though, Hallowe'en was largely |
| 15 | dying out in England. (The Irish and the Scots continued to |
| 10 | celebrate it though.) The English Hallowe'en was largely |
| 11 | absorbed into the Bonfire Night celebrations. |

In those two paragraphs I used a most effective link, 'It was then only a short step ...' (It was so effective that the editor joined the paragraphs together.) In the first paragraph I toyed with the need to put quotation marks around 'real ghosts', for how does one differentiate? But I decided that this was unnecessary – which is another useful rule of thumb for applying to punctuation: only punctuate where it helps the reader's understanding.

Note the sub-editing in the second paragraph. The word 'though' has been deleted twice. On reflection I think the first should have been left in, but the deletion of the second is an improvement – I had used it unnecessarily.

Having started the article with the American involvement in Hallowe'en celebrations I came back to it in the penultimate paragraph.

> Hallowe'en flourished in America after it was taken there in the
> 20  1840s and their 'trick-or-treat' customs were developed.
> Brought back by US service men in the 1939-45 war, the
> American way of Hallowe'en has since then been regaining
> 23  popularity in England. Few houses today are safe from
> 11  occasional 'trick-or-treat' visitations.

> The Lord Samain would no doubt turn in his grave – if only
> 23  time would once again stand still, for just the one night. Or
> 5  perhaps it still does?

Notice the short punchy final paragraph – and observe how the editor has varied my punctuation. The exchange of the dash after 'grave' for a full stop is a definite improvement but I still prefer my full stop after 'night' to the editor's dash. The phrase ends the article with just a hint of Hallowe'en fear.

The editorial changes that were made were all relatively minor; clearly the editor didn't think there was a lot wrong with my writing style. And such changes are the editor's absolute prerogative. Banish any ideas that your choice of words and style is in any way sacrosanct. The paymaster has the last word.

And finally, in this example, see how it meets my own standards of easy readability. The article is 617 words long, sufficiently close to my 600-word target. The average sentence length is under sixteen words: if I count (as I would) phrases bounded by semi-colons the sentence length comes down to just over fourteen. The longest sentence unbroken by a colon or semi-colon is 27 words long; most of the longer sentences are only 22 or 23 words long.

Even in the printed version, despite paragraph-linking, the average paragraph length is only 77 words; as submitted, it was 47 words. There are only a handful of words more than three syllables long; to the best of my belief there are no 'difficult' words at all. (As already mentioned, 'denizen' is one that I would hesitate to use in everyday speech, but it was right in this context.)

Throughout, I wrote simply and concisely – as if I were talking to a friend over the garden fence. I avoided any literary pretensions and just told what I knew. Given the material and the ideas, anyone can write like this – and sell the result.

# 6

## ILLUSTRATING YOUR ARTICLES

Look at any magazine or newspaper, and think back to the market research chapter: many articles are illustrated. If you can offer an editor a selection of *relevant* illustrations together with your article – a package deal – the editor's job is made easier. You may thereby sell more articles.

Pictures will often help your articles to sell; conversely, if you are already selling photographs, articles will help to sell your photographs. Do not get *worried* about providing illustrations, though – many articles are sold without them. Illustrations are just a bonus to article-writers. In any case, there are many organizations – trade associations, tourist bureaux, firms seeking publicity, etc. – which will provide a writer with useful photographs free of charge.

If you are interested in illustrating your articles, but have no photographic expertise, this chapter will set you on the right lines. Photography today is easier than it ever was. You need do little more than compose the picture and release the shutter.

## Types of picture

What sort of picture is bought by magazines? The way to find the answer to that question is to look again at various magazines.

Certainly, most popular and up-market magazines now use a lot of colour pictures. But many of the more 'back of the magazine' type general interest articles are still illustrated in black and white. At least initially, these are the very articles the beginning article-writer is most likely to contribute. So ... you must learn to take black and white photographs.

Overwhelmingly too, most pictures published in magazines and papers are of people or things relevant to the article they illustrate. (That's what is meant by *illustrating*.) Outside of the news pages of the daily papers there are few 'news' pictures. Equally, apart from occasionally on the editorial/leader page, there are almost no 'artistic' pictures of the camera club competition variety.

If a leading politician has a spectacular accident right in front of your camera, by all means take a photograph or twenty – and rush the film, unprocessed, to a newspaper office. Do not, though, try to compete with staff photographers at, for instance, a sporting event. They get the vantage points to photograph from; they have the equipment and the processing facilities to meet the editorial deadlines. You cannot compete.

Similarly, do not strive to take the sort of photographs that win camera club competitions. Put aside ideas of picturing back-lit drops of rain on a cobweb-draped twig. Don't try too hard to be artistic. Even if your photography does eventually extend into taking pictures to sell for their attractiveness, you will probably be most successful taking naturally attractive landscapes.

And, last of the 'do nots', don't bother to seek out spectacularly attractive girls to adorn your photographs. Although the daily tabloids are full of such pictures, they are usually commissioned – or covert advertisements. 'Girlie' pictures are not needed as illustrations to general interest articles. And they could be counterproductive.

So ... forget news pictures, club-competition-winning pictures and pictures of scantily-clad girls. Your article illustrations will often be still-life pictures: pictures of gates, bells, antiques, etc. You will be most concerned with the interest of the subject. A picture of an amusingly misshapen carrot will nearly always sell – especially if the misshape has a hint of 'naughtiness' about it. So too will pictures of road signs or advertisements that become amusing by virtue of their setting. (A signpost to 'World's End' alongside a 'No Through Road' sign is the sort of juxtaposed photograph that will often sell.)

A good market for the single picture of the curious carrot or the silly sign is the 'Odd Snap' spot found in many magazines. Watch out for such opportunities, they often pay quite well – for either black and white or colour snaps.

Another large proportion of your general interest article illustrations will be pictures of buildings, trees, castles or street-scenes. There is no overwhelming need for your picture of such scenes to be 'different'. An editor will usually prefer a conventional picture of Blanktown Castle to, for instance, a close-up of a broken battlement against a stormy black sky. (But you might sell the two pictures together – so don't pass up any different or unusually attractive shot you 'see'.)

The balance of the photographs suitable for illustrating articles will be those of people or animals. Readers like pictures of people: people *doing something* – even just dozing in a deck-chair. And pictures of animals will often outsell 'people pictures' – particularly if they are a wee bit unusual.

In a nutshell then, the photographs that you take to illustrate your articles must be of interesting subjects. The subject of the photograph is of far more importance than the artistry. And whenever possible and appropriate, some human interest should be included.

## Equipment

Before we go on to discuss how to take a saleable picture, let us consider the equipment needed. You need not bankrupt yourself. The basic equipment is just a camera and a length of film. It is seldom worth processing your own films or enlarging your own pictures – certainly it is not essential.

First then, the camera. And remember that we are talking now about an article-writer who merely wants to take occasional photographs to accompany general interest articles. Someone with little photographic knowledge or expertise – and perhaps not a lot of interest either. We are not talking about the needs of a Photographer with a capital P.

A 'compact' 35mm camera – preferably with a zoom lens and a close-up facility – with a built-in flash will satisfy all the needs of the 'ordinary' article-writer. Today, such cameras come complete with 'auto-everything' – automatic film identification, automatic focusing, automatic flash when necessary, automatic film wind-on and rewind. *All the user has to do* is 'frame' the picture and click the shutter.

A little explanation may be helpful. Many (Most? Virtually all?) of today's cameras use 35mm film. The 35 mm measurement is the width of the film; it comes in long rolls sufficient for taking 20, 24 or 36 pictures (exposures); the length of film is contained in a small light-tight cassette; after each exposure, the camera automatically pulls a fresh length of film out into place. When all the film in the cassette has been exposed it is – sometimes manually, sometimes automatically – wound back inside the light-tight cassette and can then safely be removed from the camera ... and sent for processing.

A zoom lens enables the camera to photograph a view varying from wide-angle to telescopic; most zoom lenses on compact cameras also permit close-up views of small objects – flowers, stamps, etc. The different views that the camera is taking are reflected by various different frames in the viewfinder: which will not be precise in their definition of the view, but are usually good enough.

More sophisticated (and usually far more expensive) 35 mm cameras enable the user to view the picture *through the lens* before the exposure is made. These are known as single-lens reflex (SLR) cameras: they can have a number of interchangeable zoom and other lenses (extra close-up or extra telescopic, for example). Many of today's 35 mm SLR cameras can also be used, if wished, in as automatic a manner as the compact cameras.

Both 35 mm compact and SLR cameras can, of course, use either black and white or colour film. Many professionals, particularly in the news field, take colour photographs on their 35 mm cameras. For non-news colour illustrations however, many magazines prefer the photographs to have been taken on cameras using larger-sized film – 120 roll-film. To produce colour illustrations on 120 film the photographer would probably use extremely sophisticated and expensive equipment – the Hasselblad camera springs to mind. If you are contemplating such photography ... you need expert help in choosing the equipment and learning the techniques.

Back to the recommended 'compact' camera: the best book on how to use it is ... the instruction book that comes with it. It will tell you all you need to know – and you need to know all it tells you. The more familiar you are with the operation of your camera, the less you have to think about when using it. You must be able to concentrate on the picture – not on the machinery. Practice: film's (relatively) cheap.

## Film and processing

If you are really serious about linking photography to your article-writing, you should use black and white film in your camera. The trouble with that advice is that: firstly, black and white film is hard to find – it's no longer the 'happy snap' medium; and secondly, it's more expensive to have processed – ditto. If you are intending to supply black and white photographs to illustrate your articles though – and usually this is still the sensible approach – you will be wise to use black and white film. At a pinch, black and white prints can be produced from colour negative film – but their quality can be inferior to black and white prints from black and white film.

Most of your pictures will be taken without rush or panic, in good light, often out of doors. You can therefore standardize on a moderate speed black and white film that will produce pictures of relatively fine grain. ('Grain' refers to the dots of silver compound which make up a photographic negative. Course grain can mean a print with noticeable dots. Fine grain, the opposite.) I suggest a film of around 100-200 ISO, such as Kodak Plus-X or Ilford FP4. An alternative is the differently-based Ilford XP1/XP2 film which has a faster speed, but is still fine-grained and although black and white, can be processed as colour negative film.

The processing of black and white film is a slight problem: few of the major mail-order or High Street film processing firms handle black and white film; you will need to find a specialist black and white processor. Investigate – and test – black and white processors in the classified advertisement columns of the photographic magazines.

If you progress from simple black and white photographs illustrating general interest articles – into travel features, for instance

– you need to think about colour photography. You can still use a 35 mm camera – but you'll need to use colour *transparency* film. A few magazines may still insist on Kodachrome film, most will now accept other – faster – makes. If you get into this situation, check their requirements with the relevant magazine before taking the pictures.

## Taking photographs

You have your camera, it is loaded with film, and you want to take pictures. But you've never used a camera in earnest before. Your experience has been limited to taking 'happy snaps'.

Before you dash out to take your first set of pictures it may be useful to look at your old 'happy snaps'. Or if you haven't any, think of those that you have been shown by your friends. And this time look, or think back, hyper-critically. What are the faults of most 'happy snaps' – apart from the sheer, oh-so-boring quantity? In random order – for it is difficult to decide which is the least important – most beginners' faults include:

● a generally 'messy' picture, the subject of which is not obvious;
● the subject is too small in the picture ('That's Aunt Dollie there at the back, by that bush.');
● missing – ie, cut off – 'heads and tails';
● a 'fuzzy', unsharp picture – which fuzziness can be due to either subject movement, camera movement, or improper focus;
● always horizontal ('landscape') pictures, even for vertical ('portrait') subjects.

Now consider the picture needs of editors. We have already remarked that editors are not greatly concerned with artistry. What then do they want? They simply want the illustrations to be:

● big
● clear

● sharp

and if possible,

● lively.

A comparison of the two lists shows the problem. Now the solution.

The first rule for taking acceptable, saleable, photographs is simple. It is far too often forgotten, yet it is the most important rule of all – and it's equally applicable to black and white and colour photography. It is:

## DECIDE ON THE SUBJECT

If you are taking a picture of a church weathervane, you must concentrate the camera's attention on ... the weathervane. You should not – for this purpose – photograph the weathervane complete with steeple, church, graveyard and lych-gate, however attractive the resultant picture may be. (Photograph the 'church complete' by all means – it sounds attractive – but then store it away until you want one of the church, not the weathervane.)

'Concentrate ... on the weathervane.' Do this by filling the picture with weathervane.

Filling the picture with a subject perhaps thirty metres above the ground is of course easier said than done. It could entail the use of a telephoto lens which maybe you haven't got. Use your zoom lens at its longest extreme of course – but this may still not fill the picture with weathervane. So, when you get the negatives back from processing, order an enlargement of part of the negative, concentrating on the weathervane. With the fine-grain film recommended, such part-enlargements are perfectly feasible.

Had you been photographing a small antique, a dog with a bone, or the 'church complete', it would have been easier to fill the picture with the subject. The second rule of saleable photography is now obvious:

## MOVE IN CLOSE

Don't worry overmuch about placing the subject artistically (which probably means off-centre) within the bounds of the picture. The editor is quite likely to trim off 'all that waste space'. Just move in close – either physically or with the zoom lens – and make sure that the subject fills the picture.

Getting close to a subject is of considerable assistance in ensuring that the picture is clear. There can be no doubt about what the subject is. But not every subject is suitable for ultra-close portrayal. You may have defined the subject as 'a person looking at the landscape'. (Including a person in a landscape adds valuable human interest and 'scale' to a subject often difficult to photograph well. Straightforward landscapes tend to come out too 'small', distant and unimpressive in photographs: they need something to give them scale.)

In taking pictures such as the person admiring the landscape or a fisherman mending his nets, it is essential to watch the background. Nothing makes a picture less *clear* than a confusing background. In the heat of picture-taking however, such details are often overlooked. Who, in their right mind, would ever photograph the classic picture of the tree growing from the top of a subject's head? Yet such pictures abound – because the photographer forgot at just the wrong moment.

If you seek to take photographs that will sell, you must never forget the background. The third of our rules can therefore be:

## WATCH THE BACKGROUND

The person-plus-tree is an extreme example of a poor background. The best and simplest backgrounds contrast, rather than merge, with the subject. That way, the subject automatically stands out, clearly. Simple ways of achieving this include:

● squat down so that you are looking up at the subject – this will usually provide more sky in the background. (It doesn't work so well in built-up areas though; the buildings themselves may be 'fussy' from all angles, and a tilted camera makes buildings appear to loom over.)

● stand on something so that you look slightly down at the subject – making a grassy field or the shimmering sea your background. (The high viewpoint is also suitable in towns: cobbles particularly make a fine pictorial background. They can make a good strong foreground too, from a low viewpoint.)

● a bit more technical, this one – by selective *focusing*. If you merely point your compact camera at a scene, the camera will automatically choose to focus on the generality. But if you point the camera directly at the main subject, and then half-depress the shutter-release button (to focus, and *hold* the focus) before swinging the camera back to take in the whole selected view, the resultant photograph will have the main subject sharply focused and standing out from the background which will be slightly fuzzy – soft focused. The success of this technique depends on the available lighting and on the relative positions of foreground and background. It won't always 'work' – too much light and/or too little subject-background separation will preclude it – but it's worth a try. Take other shots as well though, using different techniques, to be on the safe side.

● by contrasting lighting. Picture, for example, a musician on stage, under spotlights, against a black wall of faces. Or, if a subject is such that a silhouette is acceptable – such as a picture of a statue perhaps – photograph it against an attractive but paler sky.

The fourth rule of saleable photography is:

## GET IT SHARP

Few things detract more from a picture than the fuzziness of camera or subject movement, or of incorrect focusing. And it can sometimes be difficult to tell which of these three is the cause of a fault. Yet all can be avoided.

Few compact cameras have adjustable shutter speeds – which are the simplest way of curing camera and/or subject movement. So, if using a compact, you must find an alternative way of avoiding the shakes.

Bracing the camera against its own neckstrap is always a good idea. Wherever possible, you should also avail yourself of any natural support for the camera: hold it against a door jamb, a church's supporting column, or just a wall; rest it on a chair-back, a wall or fence-post.

Avoid attempting to photograph subjects moving rapidly across the picture, particularly if they are close to the camera; instead, try photographing them moving towards you. (Remember to get out of the way in good time though.)

Fuzzy focusing can be cured by ... careful focusing. There are few subjects appropriate to article illustration where there is no time to focus carefully. Should such an occasion arise though – the athlete racing towards you – use pre-focusing. Focus on where the action is likely to occur; wait for the subject to get there; then ... click!

The only other advice that can be offered in the form of a basic rule for tiro writer-photographers is:

## COMPOSE THE PICTURE

### Composition

Composition is a major subject. For the article-writer taking the occasional photograph to illustrate an article, let me offer just a few basic principles:

- Avoid having the subjects looking out of the picture – the reader will look elsewhere too.
- Try to frame the picture within itself – photograph the church through the lych-gate, or include a tree and its overhanging bough at the top and side of a picture. Either of these devices will tend to hold the eye within the picture.
- Arrange any action so that it moves into the picture, rather than – again – drawing the eye out of the picture.
- Avoid the centre of the picture: better, arrange the subject(s) at one or more of the one-third points. (One-third of the width in from either side and one-third of the depth away from top or bottom.)
- Ensure that the foreground contains something of interest – a person admiring the view in the background, or the main

subject of the picture, or even just old paving stones leading the eye on to the person working in the doorway.

- Use the camera vertically for upright pictures and horizontally for horizontal pictures.
- Take plenty of pictures and ruthlessly discard any that 'don't quite look right'. Professionals seldom use more than about twenty per cent of the pictures they take – and often far less.

and finally,

- Keep the picture simple; the simpler the better. Note how striking and effective are the simplest-looking advertisements; emulate them. (This takes us all the way back to the first rule – decide on the subject. Once that's done, your pictures can easily be kept simple – having strong impact.

Figure 6.1 (page 92) illustrates several of the basic principles of picture composition.

Remember too, when photographing in black and white, that you don't have the colour of a subject to make it stand out from the background. In black and white photography you have to rely on light and shade to provide the contrasts. The sun immediately behind the camera gives dull lighting – which may sometimes be right for colour photography but seldom for black and white. The sun to one side produces depth-giving shadows – except at midday, which is therefore a bad time to take any photographs. The sun in front of you, as long as your camera has the means for you to adjust the exposure to allow for it, can produce spectacular effects. But take care that the sun doesn't shine directly on to the lens.

## Picture subjects

For your writing you need to cultivate an enquiring mind, an interest in people, and some knowledge of a wide variety of subjects. Similarly, for the accompanying photographs, you should cultivate a 'seeing eye' – an eye for a good picture – and again, a variety of subjects.

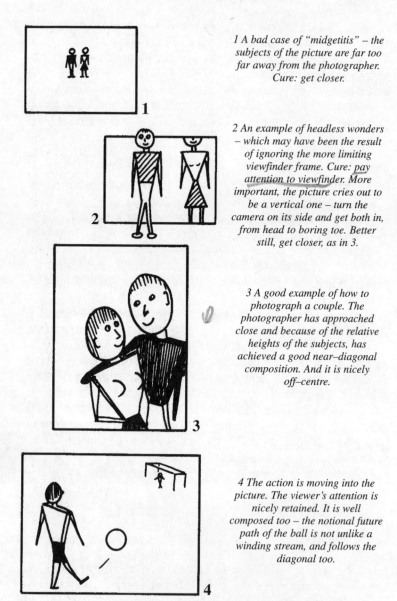

1 A bad case of "midgetitis" – the subjects of the picture are far too far away from the photographer. Cure: get closer.

2 An example of headless wonders – which may have been the result of ignoring the more limiting viewfinder frame. Cure: pay attention to viewfinder. More important, the picture cries out to be a vertical one – turn the camera on its side and get both in, from head to boring toe. Better still, get closer, as in 3.

3 A good example of how to photograph a couple. The photographer has approached close and because of the relative heights of the subjects, has achieved a good near–diagonal composition. And it is nicely off–centre.

4 The action is moving into the picture. The viewer's attention is nicely retained. It is well composed too – the notional future path of the ball is not unlike a winding stream, and follows the diagonal too.

Figure 6.1  A couple of classic photographic faults - and some examples of how to achieve 'good' composition of your photographs.

*5 Here, the back and side of a person's head in the foreground dominates the whole composition, making a comparatively "flat" landscape much more interesting.*

*6 No person in the foreground, but the tree not only dominates the foreground but also acts as a partial frame to the picture. And notice how people are included in the picture – to give it "human appeal".*

*7 The "one–third points" are here shown clearly – and illustrate how strong the resultant composition is.*

*8 The classic "intrusive background" fault. Not only does the tree sprout from the person's head but the bricks of the wall behind do not offer any contrast with the subject. But at least it's a vertical picture. Cure: move the subject (or the wall).*

*9 A good example of choice of background. Not only does the well-lit musician stand out clearly against the dark back-ground but its very darkness suggests an atmosphere very appropriate for a*

What is this 'seeing eye'? Inevitably of course, it is indefinable. It is the almost instant identification – and seizing – of the unusual, the significant, the poignant. It is what distinguishes a master photographer from a 'happy-snapper'. The seeing eye recognizes the humour in a visual situation that the man in the street passes by, unseeing. (Even the most simple or puerile humour will often suffice.) It can be the noticing of the old man's raised eyebrows as the pretty girl walks by. It can as easily be the hilarious juxtaposition of two individually staid advertising phrases – or even two conflicting traffic signs.

But the seeing eye is also the ability to make a well-composed picture of an everyday situation. If the picture is good and the composition striking, the editor may not trim in to the subject alone. This is doubly important because payment for photographs is frequently based on the size of reproduction. (But unfortunately, as we have remarked, not all editors appreciate artistic composition.)

Given the 'seeing eye', the next requirement is to build up a stock of pictures that can accompany your current and future articles. An article may need anything up to perhaps half a dozen illustrations. It may not always be convenient or possible to take all the necessary photographs at the same time as you are preparing the article. So a stock of relevant pictures is highly desirable.

Your aim should be to collect, not just single photographs, but batches of pictures about each of your chosen subjects. (See Chapter 2. Personally, I never miss an opportunity – no matter where or what I am otherwise photographing – to photograph 'new' dragons or unusual hats.)

And another hint: as and when you come across something worth photographing, take several pictures of it – from a variety of viewpoints, even if each differs only slightly. (Remember: film's cheap – and you can't always go back.) Then, if someone asks you to sell All Rights (as opposed to the normal Single Reproduction Right – see Chapter 8) in a photograph you can safely do so, while still keeping other similar pictures in your stock. If you do sell All Rights, ensure that the fee is commensurate. (It is not unusual for 'Happy Snap' competitions to require release of All Rights in winning entries.)

This advice warrants another basic photographic rule:

## DON'T JUST TAKE ONE PHOTOGRAPH – TAKE SEVERAL

As you gain experience in photography, or become more interested in it, collect batches of pictures of new subjects that interest you *pictorially*. These sets will, in turn, lead to your reading up the subject of the illustrations. Your writing will then be to accompany the pictures rather than the more usual reverse.

On occasion you may be able to sell a batch of pictures with little more written support than long captions (see below). Motoring, caravanning, cycling and walking magazines, and the like, occasionally take such features. Writing and photography complement each other particularly well too in the general interest and 'How-to' article markets. Just because you think of yourself as a writer, do not overlook occasional sales of pictures alone. As already mentioned, the 'Odd Snap' type of magazine-spot is often an attractive market.

### Other illustrations

Although you are most likely to offer black and white photographs with your early articles, there are other possibilities. Pen and ink drawings from ancient books long out of copyright can be attractive illustrations to the right article. Just be sure they are out of copyright.

If you cannot get hold of your own such ancient pictures and prints there are many picture agencies – most notably perhaps the Hulton Deutsch Collection, one of the largest in Europe, and the Mary Evans Picture Library – which will provide them ... for a fee. (See the current *Writers' & Artists' Yearbook* for an up-to-date list of picture libraries.)

If you are at all artistic yourself, you can sometimes produce your own drawings for reproduction. This is particularly appropriate for DIY features or illustrations of patterns or motifs. I have illustrated the occasional article of mine – and Figure 6.1 herein – with a careful black ink drawing on cartridge paper. (A brand new nylon-tipped pen is ideal: line width is less readily controlled with a used pen or a felt tip.)

Points to watch when making drawings for reproduction are:

- the drawing will be reproduced smaller than you draw it: ideally therefore, make your drawing twice as big as the usual illustrations in your target magazine; (minor blemishes in your drawing will happily be lost in the reduction process.)
- reduced-size reproduction means that lines too appear of reduced thickness, so do not use over-thin lines or include unnecessary detail;
- you need not 'letter up' any drawing even where this is required: provide an annotated photocopy as a key and the editor will have a staff artist finish off your drawing. An artist's lettering will be far better than yours;
- typists' correction fluid is an ideal – and, in small doses, acceptable – means of correcting your line drawings.


## Captions

And finally, a picture – photograph or line drawing – is of little value to anyone without a caption. (A caption is the description printed beneath almost every published picture.) Imagine a captionless picture of a street scene; no one would know where it was. It might almost be one of those 'Identify the holiday location in this picture' competitions. Once you explain where it is and why it is important the picture is immensely more interesting.

To ensure that you cover everything necessary in a caption, check, wherever appropriate, against the journalists' standard questions listed in Chapter 2 – my '5WH':

W – Who? –   e.g., Who is in the picture?
W – What? –   e.g., What is the person doing?
　　　　　　　and/or, What is the picture of?
W – Why? –   e.g., Why is the person doing ... whatever?
W – Where? –   e.g., Where was the picture taken?
W – When? –   e.g., When was the picture taken?
H – How? –   e.g., How is the person doing ... whatever?

Clearly, the caption for a picture of an antique artefact might only need to answer *What*? But the answer to that question might itself need to explain *Where* it came from, *When* it was made, and possibly *Who* made it, and *How*. Think about the '5WH' questions every time you write a caption; they will always be a useful guide, even though they may not all be universally applicable.

There is more photographic advice – an expansion of this chapter – in my book, *Photography for Article-Writers*, in this series.

# 7

# PRESENTATION AND SALESMANSHIP

You have now written, and polished your article; and you have long known the market to which you hope to sell it.

But the article-writing business is a buyers' market. The editor may desperately need something good to fill a two-page slot but he can always fall back on a staff-written piece or ring up one of his freelance 'regulars'. As a casual or first-time freelance you have to *persuade* the editor to buy your wares. You have to SELL your article.

Assuming that your market research (Chapter 3) has been done well, and that your article idea (Chapter 2) is a good one, you still have to present it properly. If you do not, almost irrespective of the quality of your writing, it will not sell. Presentation is an important part of article-selling.

The days when you could submit a hand-written article in an old school exercise book are long gone – if they ever existed. Your work today must be well typed. Which means that you need access to a typewriter – or a typist. And not only are paid-for typists expensive, but I have already commended to you the idea of typing your own work, amending a mangled hand-written draft as you type. So ... you need a typewriter, or better.

## Equipment

You don't HAVE to have a word processor; even a cheap manual typewriter – as opposed to a more expensive electric or electronic one – will do, at least when you start. All it needs is an 'ordinary' – either *pica* or *elit*e – typeface; avoid 'fancy' typefaces – such as mock-handwriting.

But it is certainly easier, working with a word processor. In my view, you would be wise to accumulate all your writing earnings until you can afford one. (A little more on word processors below.)

Typewriter or word processor apart, there are a few more items of inexpensive equipment that you will need to start in article-writing. They are:

- a two-hole filing punch – so that you can file correspondence and copies of output;
- a small ('Bambi' or similar) stapler to staple the pages of your articles together; (all editors are haemophiliac and object to pins – and many to paperclips too.);
- some file covers – for correspondence and copies of submitted articles (cheap lever-arch files are ideal);
- some document wallets in which to keep cuttings, notes, etc.; (or, more economically, recycle large once-used envelopes.);
- reference books – see Appendix for recommendations.

The necessary materials are a similarly small list – but they vary slightly, depending on whether you use a typewriter or a word processor. With a typewriter first:

- reasonably good quality white A4-size paper for the top copies of articles and for correspondence; (I suggest 80 gsm: too heavy a paper will send your postage bills sky-rocketing.);
- thin 'bank' (45 gsm) A4-size paper for carbon copies of articles and correspondence; (I suggest coloured paper for easy differentiation.);
- carbon paper – replace it frequently;
- typewriter ribbons (single colour, black only) – I prefer nylon ribbons, they produce a *sharper* typescript than do ordinary cotton ribbons; (Don't use 'tired' ribbons on submitted articles or correspondence – save them for drafts.);
- typists' correction fluid and correction paper.

If using a word processor the list of materials is smaller:

- reasonably good quality A4-size paper; (I use 80 gsm 'copier' paper for all purposes – other than my headed notepaper.)

● printer ribbons or cartridges. (If using a dot-matrix printer, remember to replace the ribbons freqently – use the faded ones for drafts; if using an ink-jet or laser printer, make sure you have a spare cartridge ... for when the one in use runs out.)

Now, the promised few words about word processors.


## Word processors

Basically, a word processor is a computer containing a program – a set of computer instructions – telling it how to process words. The program is either in-built, or specifically loaded into the computer; if separate, it will be on a disk.

When you write an article, letter or whatever on a word processor, your work can be 'saved' (stored) electronically onto a similar disk and reloaded (brought back on screen) at your convenience.

Associated with the word processor/computer there has also to be a printer – to transfer your 'electronic' words onto everyday paper. That's all there is to it.

When you use a word processor you type at a conventional keyboard (which has a few more keys than those on a typewriter). Your words appear on a TV-like screen in front of you. Each time you press a character-key, the character replaces the *cursor* on the screen – the cursor is merely a marker: a tiny blob or underline-mark, sometimes flashing.

One significant difference with the word processor is that you don't have to operate a carriage return lever or key at the end of each line: the words automatically move on to the next line. As far as the actual typing is concerned, you only press the 'Return' key when you want to start a new paragraph. (The 'Return' key has many more uses – in activating commands, such as 'save' or 'load', for example – but not in respect of the typing.)

Another major difference between typing on a typewriter and on a word processor is that the word processor lets you correct your typing errors or change your words at will. You merely overwrite, or insert corrections. And you can do this as often as you like. The 'last' draft is never 'finished', never immutable.

At any time you wish, you can transfer your electronically-stored words to paper; merely 'instruct' the printer to print them. You can then check your printed draft – known as a 'hard copy' – and thereafter make further corrections to the 'saved' version.

A word processor/computer plus printer need not be ruinously expensive. Computer salesmen will usually try to sell you the latest model, designed for business use: *a writer's needs are considerably less*. If you are only to write articles, a 'one-box' word-processor-plus-printer (such as the Canon, Smith-Corona or Brother) may well suffice. Next step up from that might be a dedicated 'packaged' word processor – of which 'the Amstrad' (the Amstrad PCW) was long the classic example. Probably the best buy though – if you can afford it – is a standard 'IBM-type' computer plus a separate printer. Talk to other writers – not just to computer salesmen – before you buy one; the computer world is always in a state of continuous change.

## The typescript

Whether you hand-write your article or use a word processor, it must now become a typescript. Editors require typescripts to be in a more-or-less standard format – for good reasons, as explained below.

The article must be typed (using this term to refer to output from typewriter or word processor) in double spacing with wide margins. Double-spacing means 'type a line, miss a line' – NEVER 'miss half-a-line' or what the typewriter probably has marked as 'one-and-a-half-line spacing'. Allow margins of about 40-50 mm on the left side of the page and at least 25 mm – preferably more – at top, bottom and right side.

(Using 10-characters-per-inch *pica* typeface, I set the margins at 15 and 70 spaces from the left – that is, 55 characters-width of type. When using 12-characters-per-inch *elite* typeface, I make the margins 18 and 83 giving a 65-character line. Both on A4 paper, of course.)

The double-spaced lines allow for editorial corrections and changes to your text; the margins are used for instructions to the printers.

The layout of the typescript also follows a standard form. The title of your article should be in capitals, not underlined, roughly centred on the line, about one-third of the way down the first page. Two double-spaced lines beneath that, centrally on the line, type your name in (mostly) lower-case characters – again, not underlined. Two or three double-spaced lines beneath your name, the article itself starts.

The start of the first paragraph should not be indented. Thereafter, except beneath a sub-heading, all paragraph starts should be indented by a constant amount: usually five spaces. Beneath a sub-heading, no indent for the first paragraph, thereafter the usual five.

Do not leave a line-space between paragraphs; merely start, with an indent, on the next line. If your article includes sub-headings (and this will only be when the target magazine clearly favours their use) leave a line space above and below the sub-heading – which should itself be in (mostly) lower-case characters and not underlined.

Reserve underlining exclusively for words to be printed in italics. (Mainly, book or magazine titles and foreign words; but occasionally used for an *unusual* English word – or one used unusually.) Underlining/italics is not a good way of showing emphasis. The words themselves should usually convey their importance.

When you start a fresh page you need an identifying 'strap' or 'header' in the top right-hand corner. This consists of a keyword from the article title, your name and – usually – the page number. (Some writers provide a key-word header only with the page number at the foot of the page; I think this is unnecessarily confusing. My page numbers are always in the top right-hand corner – and, with my word processor, unavoidably commence on page one.) One or two double-line spaces beneath the header, continue with the article text.

Writers with early experience in newspaper journalism often ensure that each new page starts with a fresh paragraph – which means leaving variable-sized blank spaces at the foot of each previous page. This is not necessary in article-writing – and counter-productive, making the mechanistic editorial wordage check (e.g., 10 words/line, 25 lines/page, 250 words/page) more difficult. Try, though, to avoid generating *widows* or *orphans*. (A widow is a short last line of a paragraph appearing as the first line on a new page. An orphan is the opposite – a one-line start of a paragraph at the foot of an old page.)

Another hangover from early journalistic practice is that of typing 'MF' or 'More follows' (which is its meaning) at the foot of each page except the last. This was a useful exercise when reporters sent copy to the typesetter half a page at a time; it is unnecessary when an article is delivered complete. It's obvious when there's more.

Immediately beneath the last line of the article type a short, centred burst of full-stops followed by the word END. This signifies ... the end – and saves the typesetter searching for possibly lost sheets. Further down the last page, type your name and address in full. (My own practice is also – for my own reference – to type the article's computer file name/number on the last page. No one has ever objected.) Figure 7.1 shows the layout of first and last pages of a typical article typescript.

If you are not providing a cover sheet – which I recommend, and which I come on to next – you might also, on the last page, indicate the approximate length of the article. (If no cover sheet, the word-count and your name and address also need to be on page 1 – at top right.) DO NOT specify the *exact* length of the article. For articles of under 1000 words, round off to the nearest 50; over 1000, round to the nearest 100 words.

The cover page is similar to page one. Title in capitals, centred on the line, just over a third of the way down; your name, mostly in lower-case, two or three lines further down. As before, no underlining. Then, about two-thirds of the way down the page, I always give the word count and, for convenience, the number of sheets of typescript. Something like, 'Approximately 1200 words on 6 sheets of typescript' and, when appropriate, on the next line, 'Accompanied by 0 black and white photographs (by the author) plus a separate 1-page caption sheet.'

Right down to the foot of the page now. As near to the last line as possible, ideally in the bottom left corner, type your own name and address. (And I add my computer file name/number.)

I do not, as some article-writers do, type FBSR (or, in full, First British Serial Rights) anywhere on my article typescripts.

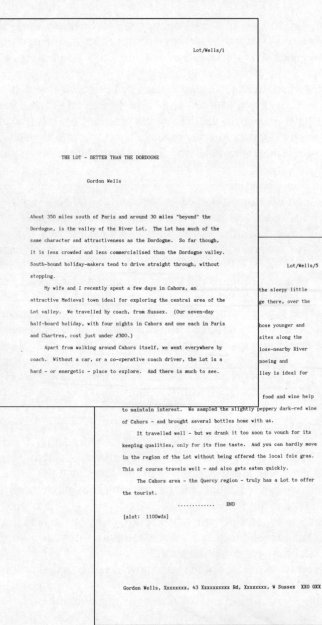

Figure 7.1  Setting out the typescript. The first and last pages of one of my articles, as submitted.

This is a necessary statement when offering short stories – because their Second, or Foreign Rights may be of value – but not with an (ordinary) article. (For a little more on Rights, see Chapter 8.)

All magazine editors assume that an article is being offered to them on a FBSR basis. If they require different – more comprehensive or wide-ranging – rights, they will tell you so. (And you just might be paid more for giving up more rights.) Usually, I would happily surrender any rights in an ordinary article; the only type of article for which I would not surrender all rights would be, for instance, an exclusive interview, which I could hope/expect to also sell elsewhere.

Other article-writers feel more strongly than I do about releasing their Rights. I believe I can always rewrite almost any article – which will usually be necessary anyway – and thereby have a fresh set of First British Serial Rights available for sale.

One supposed advantage of providing a cover sheet is that it is sometimes used by editors to arrange for your payment. And I'm all in favour of anything that facilitates payments. The editor scribbles a price on the cover sheet, separates it off, and sends it to the accounts department; after editing, the rest of the typescript goes to the typesetter. Your name and address are on both parts.

As mentioned above, I provide a caption sheet for any illustrations. This is part of, but not a continuation of, the typescript. Like the article itself, the captions should be typed double-spaced, with letters or reference numbers to link them to the correct pictures. The caption sheet(s) should also carry the article title and your name and address – again, for safety.

## Picture presentation

Editors like illustrations accompanying articles, and they like them to be big. The preferred size always used to be 10" x 8" – but with increasing costs more editors appear willing to accept prints of a smaller size. Prints sized 8" x 6" seem generally acceptable and that is the size used for prints accompanying many press releases. (I have occasionally sold articles accompanied only by standard 6" x 4" 'enprints'. These are only acceptable if the subject is big and clear in the print and they are only intended for small-size use.)

As already mentioned, the article-writer would usually be wise to have the film and print processing done commercially. Order 'selective enlargement' to 8" x 6" size, on glossy paper, *with bled edges* (that is, with no white borders). Not only do these look more professional, but you get more picture for your money. Only glossy prints are acceptable for reproduction.

Editors vary on where they prefer the captions. Some like them to be taped to the back of the pictures; others specify separate caption sheets. As already mentioned, I usually provide a separate sheet of captions but with each caption sufficiently spaced so that the caption sheet can be cut up in the editor's office if necessary. But whether the captions are attached to the pictures or separate on a caption sheet, ensure that picture and caption can be adequately associated. And – for identification purposes – the back of every print must bear your name and address. For this, as for many similar purposes, I use tiny adhesive address labels.

Photographs are liable to damage in the post. A photograph folded in two is a photograph ruined: it cannot then be used for reproduction. Photographs accompanying articles must therefore be protected. It is convenient to protect photographic prints with a piece of card fractionally larger; an elastic band stretched diagonally across two corners will hold the package together better than a paper clip. (A paper clip may also damage the prints – yet editors frequently use them.)

Figure 7.2 illustrates the best way of packing article, photographs, covering letter and return envelope for posting.

Sometimes, when you are better known to an editor, you may be able to sell him photographs as contact prints. Send the contacts with the article and the editor will specify which negatives he wants enlarged. Or he may even – if you are prepared to agree – take the negatives, have his own enlargements made, and return the negatives. All at minimal cost to you. But don't try this approach on a new editorial contact, or on the editor of a small magazine. It is only worth adopting with bigger publications with their own photographic facilities, and where you yourself are well known to them.

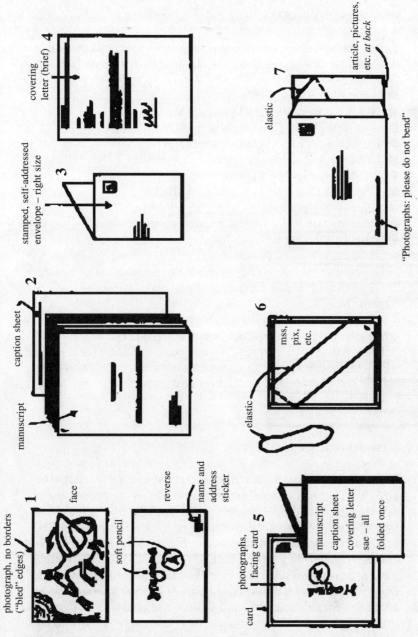

Figure 7.2 The best way of packaging an illustrated article for submission to an editor.

## Pre-despatch checklist

Before actually despatching your article, make one final check that it is as good as you can make. Work through this check list:

- Is the TITLE gripping?
- Has it a good OPENING paragraph?
- Is it the right STYLE for the market?
- Is it the right LENGTH for the market?
- Is it CORRECT in every detail?
- Is there enough MEAT in it?
- Does it FLOW smoothly – and swiftly?
- Have you cut out all UNNECESSARY words?
- Does the typescript LOOK attractive – professional?
- Would YOU buy it?

If you can answer YES to each of those questions, your article's in with a fair chance of acceptance. (If not – back to Square One.)

All is now ready for you to despatch your article, plus pictures if any, to the magazine for which it was designed. There is a school of thought that says, 'Just send it – any editor can see what it is and who it's from; he knows it's on spec and he knows you expect it to be paid for, or returned.' I think they're wrong.


## A covering letter

My own view is that an article should always be accompanied by a BRIEF covering letter. That seems no more than polite, and in accordance with normal business practice. After all, I am a salesman offering my product for sale; the editor has not always asked for it; anything that I can do to help achieve a sale is worth doing.

Let the covering letter be little more than a formality, though. The editor does not need you to tell him that the information came from such-and-such a reference book. Nor does he want you to apologize for that mass of hand-written alterations. Don't apologize: retype it. In time, as you sell more and more features to the same magazine, you may build up a working relationship with the editor: until then, confine yourself to business. (But see below for query letters – which are becoming increasingly necessary.)

My own, fairly standard, letter to an editor, covering an article submitted on spec, is along these lines:

Dear Mr/Mrs/Ms/Miss .../Bill/Bill Smith

I enclose herewith, for your consideration for publication at your normal rates, a 000-word article, 'TITLE', about SUBJECT. (... together with 00 photographs.)

If the article is accepted, I would appreciate, in addition to payment, a copy of the issue of MAGAZINE in which it appears, for my records. If it is not accepted, I would appreciate the return of the article, I enclose the customary stamped addressed envelope.

Yours sincerely

Gordon Wells

Enc: 'TITLE' MS (plus 00 pix)
s.a.e.

Points to note in the letter are:

- I write to the editor or features editor by name whenever I can. The relevant names are usually found on the magazine's contents page or in one of the Yearbooks, or in *The Magazine Writer's Handbook* – but make sure that you are using an up-to-date name from an up-to-date magazine or reference book. Additionally, or alternatively, you can usually confirm a name with the magazine's telephone operator. It is also worth noting that, throughout the publishing world, it is increasingly common to address people by their first (and last, if you don't yet know them) name, rather than the more formal Mr/Mrs, etc.
- It is worth explaining – in no more than half a dozen words – what the article is about, in case the title is not self-explanatory.
- I usually ask for a copy of the issue of the magazine in which

the article is used. This is sometimes known as a 'voucher copy'. If I don't ask, I may not get a copy. If I do ask, I still don't always get a copy: some editors forget, some have a deliberate policy of not supplying copies. (Some though, are meticulous in supplying contributors' copies.) I keep a scrap-book of my published articles.

- You should always enclose a stamped addressed envelope. The absence of one *might* mean instant unconsidered rejection. The envelope is sometimes used for rejection, sometimes to send an acceptance letter and/or the payment cheque. Make sure that the envelope is big enough to hold the material you are despatching and is sufficiently stamped for return postage. (Second-class return postage is a saving worth making: if the article is accepted, the acceptance letter will probably not need so much postage; the second-class expense often covers first-class return.)

  As and when you progress to offering articles to overseas markets, you can, if you have a word processor (permitting easy replacement of material), merely send International Reply Coupons sufficient for a simple response. Tell the editor that he need not return the article.

- And of course, the most important point of all is that it is a letter. Do not try to deliver your article personally to the editor. Editors are busy people, often working with only a few staff colleagues; they can do without visits from tiro freelance writers, usually seeking advice. If and when an editor wants to see or speak to you, he will phone. (But don't sit in waiting for the call.)

Editors would undoubtedly prefer all submissions to arrive on their desks unfolded. But A4 envelopes are expensive. And not all editors pay big money. My practice is to send longer, unillus-trated articles folded in half only, and shorter ones folded twice to fit into a DL size envelope. (DL is the size of the usual long business envelope.)

Where, for an illustrated article, I have to use a particularly large envelope, I occasionally enclose only a stamped addressed label for return. This keeps down the weight and therefore the cost of postage. No editor has yet complained.

## Timing submissions

If your article is not tied – as, for instance, my Hallowe'en one was – to a specific publication date, then when you submit it is of little consequence. But many articles are, in one way or another, time-related. It is important that they reach the editor at the right time for consideration for the appropriate issue.

It is no use whatsoever submitting an article about Christmas cards or mistletoe customs to a monthly magazine in November. (And anyway, all the 'ordinary' Christmas subjects have been done to death. You need to come up with something new.) The Christmas issue will long since have gone to the printers.

So, when should you submit your time-related articles? Ignoring Christmas for the moment, you will not go far wrong if you work to the following timetable. It allows not only for the editorial thought-process but also for the usual 'pre-date publication' practice; it does not merely indicate the last possible date before material goes from editor to printer:

| | |
|---|---|
| Daily newspapers (including evenings) | : 2-4 weeks ahead |
| Weekly magazines | : 6-12 weeks ahead |
| Monthly magazines | : 3-6 months ahead |
| Quarterlies | : 6-12 months ahead |

The 'Bumper Christmas Issue' of any magazine is probably being planned – if only in the back of the editor's mind – all year round. July is by no means too early to send your Christmas offering to either a monthly or a weekly magazine.

## Query letters

If you are contemplating a lot of – possibly expensive – research for an article it is clearly wise to check with the editor of your choice before starting. This has always been true. But in the past it was not usual to pre-check the interest of a British magazine editor in most ordinary, short articles – they were merely submitted on spec. (I have though, always checked with editors for articles of about 2,000 words or longer.)

American magazines have long insisted on a preliminary letter in advance of virtually any article manuscript. To some extent, this was an understandable reflection of the usually longer length of American magazine articles: a British short article is an American 'filler'.

The worldwide recession of the eighties however led to drastic cuts in British editorial staffs. Tighter editorial staffing means less time available for sifting through the dozens of – mostly unsuitable – unsolicited article (and short story) manuscripts in search of the occasional pearls. Accordingly, many more magazines commission most feature articles from known freelances. They refuse to even look at unsolicited submissions. But most say they will consider query letters – article ideas or outlines.

Unfortunately a number of magazines don't even bother to respond at all to what, to them, are uninteresting ideas. Yes, even when you *do* enclose the obligatory stamped addressed envelope.

(The situation is exacerbated by some magazines only being willing to consider queries accompanied by evidence of previous similar publication. How can you demonstrate to the editor of one magazine that you have had work published in similar magazines if the editors of all those similar magazines demand like evidence? It's a hard world. Luckily for tiro article-writers there are still plenty of magazines prepared to consider submissions without evidence of prior publication. The 'way in' is to gain 'lesser' acceptances and gradually work your way up.)

An editorial query must be written with care. You've got to sell your idea to a hard-pressed editor in just a few paragraphs.

There are differing views on how to query. American magazines appear to prefer a 'hard sell' approach – often within the covering letter, which then resembles a mail order *spiel*. British magazines seem to prefer a somewhat less brash approach.

My own recent practice, largely confined to broadly 'How-to' articles (see below) for magazines where I am 'known', is not necessarily valid across a broader spectrum. So I asked a number of editors of various magazines for their preferred approach. Inevitably, each had their different ideas ... but there is a broad consensus. The following specific recommendations are based on that consensus view.

Unsolicited feature article queries – which, surprisingly, most editors are willing to consider in batches of two or three ideas at a time – should:

- of course be typed (but can be single-spaced, if well laid out and easy to read);
- each be separate, preferably on a single sheet of A4 paper, and accompanied by the briefest of covering letters;
- contain a general description of the proposed article and its content – and a good suggestion for the title will help (but see below for articles of a more technical nature);
- suggest the likely length of the proposed article – while acknowledging that should the editor require a longer or shorter article, this presents no problem;
- briefly outline the writer's credentials – subject knowledge, contacts, etc. – for writing the particular article, and experience of writing similar pieces for other magazines (photocopies of similar published work – but not more than one or two pages altogether – will be helpful);
- mention whether illustrations can be provided (if already available 'from stock', perhaps enclose a photocopy of one or two);

and, of course,

- be accompanied by a stamped addressed envelope.

Figure 7.3 shows a typical general interest feature query.

The above approach to article queries is suitable for the more general interest type of article. For 'How-to' articles it is appropriate to be rather more specific in the advance details. My own practice is to suggest a title, show the opening paragraph or two (the 'hook') and then list, with 'bullet points' the broad areas of advice to be included. It works for me.

A good query – an article outline – is worth the investment of some time and thought. At the very least, it saves abortive work on the article proper.

At first approach, a new-to-you editor may only respond by saying that the idea looks good and that he'd like to see the finished article on spec. As an editor comes to know you and your work, you may occasionally get positive acceptances in

ARTICLE OUTLINE/QUERY

LEISURELY LUXOR

Gordon Wells

Lord Carnarvon had the right idea. The way to enjoy
Egypt is to take it easy. It's too hot to hurry.
        When, in 1922, the entrance to Tutankhamun's tomb
was uncovered, Lord Carnarvon was a mile away, resting
in his house. His workmen knew that, if they found
anything that looked promising, his Lordship was to be
summoned. And so he arrived, on time.
        Everyone has heard of the fabulous treasures found
in the tomb. Many were brought to Britain for the
Tutankhamun exhibition, in 1972.
        Yet Tutankhamun was not one of the really great
Pharaohs ...

Thereafter:
For a thousand years, long before the birth of Christ,
Luxor was the capital of Upper and Lower Egypt. And the
sights for today's tourist include not only the famous
tombs but also vast temples and monumental statues.

I would describe not only some of the impressive sights
but also a more 'ordinary' fiacre ride and a sail in a
felucca on the Nile - and the many Egyptian ways of
parting tourists from their small change - baksheesh.

My 'credentials' for offering this article: my wife and
I have recently enjoyed a one-week package holiday in
Luxor; we 'did' Luxor thoroughly - and I've read up
sufficient of the history. I have written a number of
similar travel articles for The Lady, and others.

I will write the article to about 1400 words plus a
small 'fact-file'. But this length can of course be
varied. The article would be accompanied by six black
and white photographs: I enclose a photocopy of one.

Given a go-ahead, I could deliver the material within
three weeks.
                ..................

Gordon Wells
Xxxxxxxx
43 Xxxxxxxxxx Road
Xxxxxxxxxxx  W Sussex  XX0 0XX

Tel/fax: 01000-000000

Figure 7.3 Layout and content of a typical one-page, general interest
query/outline for submission to an editor

advance, based on your outlines. Don't expect such firm go-aheads until the editor knows you well though – and even then, you won't always get one.

But an invitation to submit on spec is 'nearly there'. Work hard on the article, make it a good one and get it in as soon as possible – not forgetting to remind the editor of his invitation/interest.

## Sell a series  *with days*

Finally, there is one thing even better than selling an article to an editor – and that is selling a whole series of articles as yet unwritten. You will not achieve this happy state with your first few published articles, but you should always keep your antennae tuned for series opportunities.

When offering the editor of a monthly 'trade' magazine an article on letter-writing, I suggested that it might usefully be extended into a series on business communication – telephone techniques, oral presentation, etc. I did no more than list a number of linked topics. The editor assessed my style and treatment from the initial article; liked it – and the idea of the series; and said yes. I'd sold half a dozen articles rather than just the one.

Think back to the ideas on professionalism that I expounded in Chapter 1. By selling that series on communication techniques I 'saved' myself about thirty to forty per cent of the normal work: I did the whole of the market research and salesmanship just once, on the initial article.

Any series is regular work ... and regular money too. And the rate of pay for a series is often better than for 'one-offs'.

Always keep your eyes open for series opportunities. After all, when you suggest such an idea, what have you to lose? The worst that can happen is that the editor turns you down. But be sure to work it all out carefully before you make an offer. If you fall down on a regular commitment the editor will not be pleased.

# 8

## BUSINESS MATTERS

It doesn't matter that you are only writing in your spare time; from the moment that you start trying to sell your articles, you are 'in business'. And you need to be businesslike about it. You need to keep records of your output – and where each article is – and you will have to keep account of your expenditure and earnings.

At the same time, you are a writer, not a book-keeper. What you need is the least time-consuming method possible of keeping records and accounts. The less time that is spent on business matters, the more time there is for productive writing.

I have already mentioned, in the previous chapter, one of the first aspects of being businesslike: your letters to editors. But I did not then mention the notepaper. You will be operating in a business world where all letters are typed, usually on A4 paper, and always on headed paper. As you start to sell your articles more frequently, you too need to invest in headed notepaper.

This needs to look professional – not amateurish. Don't go in for anything too 'pushy', nor too 'twee'. Leave large flamboyant headings to the local shopkeepers: leave flowery script headings to society ladies. Have good quality white A4 paper printed with your name and address, in the simplest, plainest type. Not too large. And in my view, there is no need to say 'Author' or 'Freelance writer' or whatever in the heading. It should be obvious.

(If you have a word processor program which enables you to design and preserve your own standard letter heading, this can be a big saving. Again though, the same advice: keep it 'ordinary'. Resist the temptation to add in a bit of that free 'graphic art'; don't use an unusual typeface. Make the heading plain and simple – and to your taste. Then stick to it. Resist all temptations to change it.)

## Keeping records

Even before you invest in headed notepaper you will need to start keeping records of which article you have sent where – and with what result. The system that I use, I have simplified again and again; I think it is now as simple as possible, while recording all that I need to know.

I now maintain my record solely on my computer: I no longer bother with a 'hard copy'. But the same method will work equally well on a hand-written sheet of narrow-lined A4 paper, ruled into columns. Either way, the columns are headed:

- article number
- file
- title
- number of words and pictures
- magazine sent to (and date)
- accept/reject (and date)
- date published
- date paid
- amount paid

Nowadays, having produced a considerable number of articles over the years, I give each article a five-digit number. Even for those just starting, I commend this approach: it's easy to start off with and, as I discovered, hard to back-track later to renumber.

The first three digits of my number represent the year. Thus, 967 means the year commencing 6 April 1996. (For accounting convenience, I organize all my work around standard financial years.) Then I allocate a two-digit number to each article written during that year. For example, the ninth article written in year 96/7 is numbered 96709. (I've not yet written more than 99 articles in any year. But I do write books as well.)

A numbered 'hard copy' of each article is stored, in running order, in a lever-arch file. I can always find a copy quickly.

I also keep an electronic copy of each article on computer disk, in case I need to run off another copy or rewrite it for another market.

It is most convenient for the computer copy to have some sort

117

of identifying name – which is also written on the hard copy. The actual article title is usually too long – computer file names are (usually) restricted to eight characters. I write all sorts of things other than articles. So – all articles have file names commencing with A and up to seven other letters: a key word from the title – in full or abbreviated – or a series name plus a number or date.

Thus, an article about ... keeping records, called *Keeping tags* is filed as ATAGS; one of my regular *A Problem Shared* columns for *Writers' Monthly* is filed as AWMQ0995 (which translates, to me, as the *WM* 'Questions' article for September 1995). Before I had a hard disk on my computer, I added the disk number – e.g. ATAGS.31 – to my recording of the file name. (But not to the file name itself; it would be pointless to add the same number to each file on the disk.)

The other columns in my record sheet are straightforward: I record the number of words and illustrations to facilitate comparing payment rates; I record submission and acceptance/rejection dates so that I can investigate any extra-long decision times; also publication and payment dates so that I can chase overdue payments.

If an article is rejected, I use the remaining columns to indicate where it is next offered. It retains its same number, name and title for its second (and any subsequent) submission.

When maintaining this record sheet manually, I circled the A in the accept/reject column in green ink. (A green pen just happened to be handy when I started the system.) This was so that the acceptance-fact stood out. It's good for morale. Nowadays, with far fewer rejections, I highlight the R on my computer screen: appropriately, it shows up blue.

From a glance at the submissions sheet I can quickly see which editorial decisions are outstanding – and for how long. Occasionally, I send a polite 'chaser' letter; most often, I just wait. You are better employed putting together a new article than chasing an old one.

Previously, but no longer, I kept a second sheet recording the several magazines to which each article was sent. Even more now than in the past, articles are better rewritten before being offered elsewhere: a fresh, accurately-targeted article for each submission.

The longer you maintain records such as I have outlined above, the more you realize three truths about editors:

- Editors seldom waste time writing letters – but sometimes, if you are lucky, they will telephone.
- Some editors dislike making decisions about submitted articles before they need to use them. (But they quickly reject all unsuitable work, so no news is often good news.)

The third 'truth' is really the second one rephrased. It is, though, worth mentioning:

- Editors often hold on to work for quite a while before they use it – or reject it.

It is sound business sense to keep a written note of any telephone discussions with an editor. He may, for instance, agree with you on a price for your work – and then, probably inadvertently, forget what was agreed. This happened to me; I reminded the editor of our telephone agreement and got an instant apology – closely followed by a further cheque to top up the unintentional underpayment. I don't trust my memory on such matters: I ALWAYS make a note.

But with editors so loth to put pen to paper, how do you know if your work has been accepted or rejected – or just lost?

The only answer, I fear, is that you will gradually get to know different editors' response-patterns. Almost all magazines will reject completely unsuitable material within about a month. Many magazines will confirm acceptance, too, within about a month; but some expect the writer to interpret non-rejection as 'possible acceptance – the material is being held for possible use some time in the future'. Some magazines, luckily only a few, just never reply at all, stamped addressed envelope or no.

It is all most unsatisfactory – but there is little any one writer can do about it. And of course, you will seldom be paid for a 'retained' article until it is actually published.

## Keeping accounts

Mention of payment leads us conveniently on to the need for the writer to keep accounts. The writer needs to keep financial accounts for two reasons:

- to ascertain whether or not he is making money,
- to satisfy the Tax Inspectors (and minimize his tax liability).

Your article-writing may be no more than an occasional hobby; you may – unbelievably – not care whether or not you make a profit; but you should KNOW. You may be making good money from some of your writing activities, while making disastrous losses on another aspect. If you have that information you can (should) concentrate your activities on the profitable activities. (Or identify economies in the loss-makers.)

Think about the cost of writing. Stationery and postage are the major ongoing expenses and they will not vary much with different types of writing. It is your time and your research activities that vary with each article. And you are probably not bothering to record all of those expenses.

The time and money spent on research can be considerable. It may not be a good – i.e., worthwhile – investment. Before starting the subject research for an article, think about the economics: you can easily spend, say, £25 on research (postage, travel, photocopies, etc.) for a small feature article. If the article is going to sell for about £50-60 it might just be worth the while – but suppose the article is rejected? (And it happens to all of us on occasions.) It could be a complete waste of money.

If however you can use the same research for several articles with a total earning potential of several hundred pounds ... the research expenditure is well justified. It's difficult to be precise about research costs and the like, but it is always worth thinking about costs and possible returns before starting.

(I've recently been asked to write a thousand-word 'profile' of an American sports personality; I'm finding it difficult to collect the necessary background material. The payment on offer is limited – so I may turn the job down. And I don't often do that.)

Just as keeping records of submissions and acceptances is important to the writer, so too is the keeping of accounts. But, to repeat, you are a writer, not a book-keeper. So the book-keeping should be simple ... and minimized.

I have developed a simple yet complete system – it is strictly 'Low Tech'; I don't use my computer for it, at all. I use a ready-ruled Accounts Book with a 'date' column, a 'details' column and 14 'cash' columns – across a two-page spread. The first two cash columns are used for total receipts (with a letter to categorise: A articles, B books, etc.) and expenditure; then I break down the many small expenses.

The next five columns *repeat* (and split up) the expenditure, under a number of classifications – which are particularly helpful when I am completing my annual Income Tax return:

- postage (always a major expense)
- research (books, magazines, library order fees, etc.)
- stationery (including photocopies, films and processing)
- travel (ticket costs or mileage costs for car travel)
- others (telephone costs, conferences, etc.)

And, because I don't only write articles, in the last several columns across the double-page I *repeat* the expenditure *again*. This second time, it is categorized by writing activities: articles, books, lectures, etc. I can thus compare my earnings from, say, lecturing with the expenses thereof. At first, this second break-down of expenses will probably be inappropriate; in time, though ... So bear it in mind.

(It is important that you do not neglect to declare even small writing earnings to the Tax Inspector: apart from anything else, you're likely to get caught out – magazines have to declare their payments. Furthermore, if you keep proper accounts right from when you start freelancing, you will be allowed to claim reasonable past expenses against early future earnings. As a guide to your own dealings, the Tax Inspector has, at various times, accepted my claims for: telephone rental for incoming calls, and self-assessed call-by-call costs for outgoing calls (and faxes); car mileage at reasonable rates; and a small, regular payment to my wife for clerical and research assistance. But be fair and honest with the Tax people: your expenses must be real – not 'notional'.)

Value Added Tax (VAT) is another form of taxation. As an article-writer it is unlikely that your *turnover* – which is what VAT is levied on – will approach the minimum VAT-registration level.

And the small amount of VAT that an article-writer could reclaim is unlikely to warrant the book-keeping work of maintaining VAT records and returns.

## Other markets

Many writers eventually extend their activities beyond their initial interests. I started with photography and began writing articles to help sell the photographs; it wasn't long, though, before the writing became more important. Then for a while, I concentrated on non-fiction book writing, leaving little time for articles or photography. Nowadays, I work on non-fiction books and articles at the same time – and I write fiction and non-fiction for children too. As a result of one of my other-than-writing books, I became involved in lecturing (to engineers). I have also done some publicity work, writing brochures, etc. If it involves writing or speaking, I'll have a go. So can you.

Not all writing and associated activities entail the use of the same techniques though. Just as, in this book, you have been learning the craft – the techniques – of article-writing, so too do other techniques have to be learnt.

Writing a non-fiction book is a logical next step for many successful article-writers – but the approach is very different.

Anyone serious contemplating writing a non-fiction book is referred to my book *How to Write Non-Fiction Books* in the Allison & Busby Writers' Guides series. (It is a totally updated and rewritten version of my earlier book T*he Successful Author's Handbook* [Papermac, 1981/1989]) In a nutshell though, the basic differences between article-writing and book-writing are:

● you sell the idea for the book to a publisher before you write much of it. (The 'sales package' that you offer to a publisher consists initially of a synopsis – to produce which you need to be really well *organized* – and a brief description of objectives, market, etc. Later, you show an interested publisher one or two sample chapters. Only when you have a contract for the book do you write the rest.)

122

- you can expand – extend yourself – in a book. (You are no longer restricted to a thousand-word subject for a thousand-word article. It is more important that the subject is fully covered.)
- you will be much more involved in the production and sales process. (You will, for instance, always have to check proofs before the book goes to the printer. You may be asked to assist in the selling process – perhaps including radio, or even TV, appearances.)
- you will probably wait even longer for your money. (Payment – other than advances – will be on a royalty basis, paid six-monthly or annually in arrears, on sales over the past period.)

If you do sell-and-then-write a book on your specialist subject, you will become a more *credible* article-writer. It will be worth mentioning your book on article title pages. When writing articles about management communication techniques, I used to add, beneath my name, 'Author of *How to Communicate* (McGraw-Hill, 1978/1986)'. (This is no longer a valid credit-line: the book 'ran its course' with McGraw-Hill; the rights reverted to me – and I sold it again, as a third edition, retitled *Effective Communication* to a Singapore-based publisher.) Apart from suggesting to the editor that my article was likely to be authoritative, this note may have helped to sell one or two more copies of the book – earning me my ten per cent on each sale.

## The writer's scrapbook

Every writer should keep a scrapbook. When you are feeling depressed, sure that you will never again be able to write another saleable word, a browse through your past successes will re-inflate your ego. But ego-trips – important though they undoubtedly are – are not the only justification for keeping a scrapbook.

Your scrapbook will also help spark off ideas for new articles, new versions of old articles, or wholly new subjects. Your scrapbook is an excellent reference source too. You know that you did your research properly in the first place; you can quickly pick out the facts you need, and write them up again – differently – for a new feature.

Buy as large a scrapbook as possible. No matter how big it is, many newspaper articles will be too big to fit in to a page. Most multiple stationers sell scrapbooks – choose the one with the least garish cover. A scrapbook is money well spent. (My scrapbooks now run into more than twenty volumes – but that's not only articles, there are picture stories and book covers too. Looking back at one's earliest published work is salutary too – however did it get accepted?)

## Business questions and answers

● *Do I need an agent?*
No. You should deal with editors yourself. Editors are accustomed to direct contact with writers. In any case, few if any agents would be prepared to take on an article-writer as a client. Agents make their living from a (ten to fifteen per cent) commission on all of their clients' sales: most individual article sales earn too little to pay for an agent's time. An agent usually only handles articles as a favour to a client whose other earnings – from books, etc. – justify his involvement.

● *What rights am I selling? (And what are 'rights' anyway?)*
Normally – unless you specify otherwise – you are offering first magazine reproduction rights when you submit an article to a magazine. Some writers mark their MS (the standard abbreviation for a single manuscript – the plural is MSS) 'FBSR', meaning 'First British Serial Rights' but I always let this be assumed. Merely by offering it, you are saying that the article is your own work and has not already been published elsewhere. (Of course, if the article *has* been published elsewhere, then you must say so. See below.) The word 'Serial' refers to a 'serial publication', i.e. a magazine.
The magazine in turn is only buying the 'right' to publish the article once. Should they wish to re-use it – in, for instance, an annual – they must pay for it again.
The significance of *First* rights is that some smaller magazines are prepared to take second rights and re-use an already

published article. But when you can rewrite the article to use much the same facts in a different way, and thereby again sell first rights – at first rights rate of pay – second rights are largely academic to an article-writer. (Second rights are much more important to a writer of short stories – stories are often sold more than once, unchanged.)

*First Rights* mean exactly what the word says – FIRST. Even if an article is only published in a club, or other small-circulation magazine, the *First Rights* have gone ... whether paid for or not.

When offering a once-published article, unamended, to a magazine in a foreign country you can still offer, for instance, 'First American Serial Rights' – but it is customary to point out that First British Serial Rights have already been sold. (Some major magazines on both sides of the Atlantic will, not unreasonably, ask for 'First World Rights'. No problem – you can rewrite. Some may ask for '*All* Rights'. As far as possible, this should be avoided; you might later wish to re-use the material unchanged, in, for instance, a book. If a magazine insists on All Rights, try for a commensurate payment. But don't be too insistent; again, you can always rewrite.

● *What about copyright?*
Your work is copyright as soon as you commit it to paper. The FBSR, etc., to which we have been referring above is, in fact, a release of your copyright for the one use specified.

It is important for an article-writer to understand just what is, and what is not, copyright. There is no copyright in ideas, titles or facts, only in the way in which they are presented. That is why I could explain above that if you sell First British Serial Rights, you can re-write the article and sell it again – as First Rights.

There is then the need to differentiate between infringement of copyright and plagiarism. The easy, albeit flippant, answer to that is the advice I was given long ago: 'If you read up a subject in one book and write about it – that could be plagiarism: if you read two books – that's research.' You must never merely rewrite the whole or part of *someone else's* work.

The average article-writer however, collects facts from a variety of sources and then puts a batch of them together in his own – uniquely interesting – way. If he uses a different mixture of many of the same facts, possibly in a different sequence, the result is a wholly new article – in which the copyright is his.

● *Does FBSR, etc. apply to photographs too?*
No. When you offer a – black and white or colour – photograph to an editor, usually but not exclusively accompanying an article, you are merely offering the right to a single reproduction. Not necessarily the first use, nor do you need to mention any previous uses. And the magazine may not re-use the photograph without a further, single-use payment. And even if an editor asks for any other right – sometimes 'All Rights' are asked for – you should normally refuse unless extremely well compensated. (You might well wish to sell 'World Rights' in a spectacular news picture – for a spectacular fee.)

It is against the possibility of being asked to relinquish all rights in a photograph that I earlier recommended taking several photographs of each subject. It is also a safety precaution for competition-material 'Happy Snaps'.

● *Can I sell articles to overseas magazines?*
There is no reason why not – so long as you direct your submission to appropriate publications. (My own articles have appeared – occasionally – in magazines in America, Hong Kong, Singapore, and Australia.) Market research is as important when selling overseas as it is for home sales – more so, because postage costs are greater. Enclose return postage for overseas magazine editors in the form of International Reply Coupons, obtainable from any Post Office. (Each IRC can be exchanged, in the overseas country, for stamps to the minimum cost of return airmail letter post.) Remember though that many overseas editors expect a query letter before consideration of any article. It is also worth bearing in mind that the ease of printing out another copy of a word-processed article means it's probably not worth asking for the return of a rejected MS.

● *Need I really bother about accounts and tax matters if I only write two or three articles a year?*
Probably not – but at the same time, you cannot claim any expenses against your writing. But whether or not you bother to keep accounts, you should not neglect to declare any payments you receive – for even two or three articles a year. Be assured that the Tax Inspector will know of your earning: editors report all payments.

● *How much does article-writing pay?*
This is a 'how long is a piece of string?' question. At the lower end of the scale, some magazines pay no more than about £20 per thousand words – and *pro rata*. Against that, some of the really top markets will pay hundreds of pounds per thousand words. In the middle, maybe £50-70 per thousand words is about average.

A spare-time article-writer with a wide range of interests and knowledge might be able to produce about one 1000-word article each week. But this is not a typical spare-time writer; most will not have a sufficient breadth of knowledge to maintain this output. They will need to make time for research – and for thinking up ideas.

But let's assume that you *could* produce one article a week – you would probably sell one in two. And they would be the type of article likely to sell in the lower to middle range of markets. So ... 26 thousand-word articles per year, selling at between £20 and £100 each earns £1500 a year. A spare-time writer would be lucky to make that much. And there are expenses to come off that figure.

As you gain in competence and experience, you may be able to write for the higher-paying magazines and also to increase your percentage of sales to output. Maybe. Moving 'up-market' often means more time on research and fewer sales, at least initially.

● *Should I take up article-writing as a full-time occupation?*
Another 'piece of string' question. Undoubtedly there are those who work full-time at article-writing and presumably, some must make a good living at it. For the more 'ordinary', more

127

average – more nervous – article-writer, it must depend on whether or not you like to eat well and regularly. Also on your self-confidence.

If you are making £1000-a-year from ten hours a week spare-time writing and can maintain the flow of ideas and words for, say, fifty hours a week ... that gives you £5000 per annum.

I work full time at writing and associated activities – but I should hate not to have my pension to provide the bread and butter on which to spread the 'jam' of my writing income.

# APPENDIX

# A LIBRARY FOR THE ARTICLE-WRITER

Every writer needs reference books; an article-writer probably needs more reference books than a writer of fiction. Reference books are the first - and second, third and fourth - sources for every new article. Some reference books are of general application to all article-writers and it may help the reader if I list my own favourites. The list is not particularly comprehensive - it just suits me.

## General reference books

● A dictionary. Mine, sitting on the shelf immediately in front of my desk, is *The Concise Oxford Dictionary* (Oxford University Press: 6th edition, 1978) and it is in constant use. (I also make a lot of use of the 'family dictionary', the *Longman Dictionary of the English Language* [Merriam-Webster Inc./Longman, London, 1984]).

When I am *quite sure* how to spell a word, I always look it up - and far too often I find that my certainty was misplaced. (Only the other day I was prepared to swear that 'loquacious' was spelt with a 't' instead of a 'c' - and I went for years believing 'desparate' to be the correct spelling of 'desperate'.) It pays to check spellings frequently.

● *The Oxford Writers' Dictionary* (Oxford University Press: Oxford, 1990). Not the same as an 'ordinary' dictionary but essential for the writer: it offers authoritative advice on which alternative spellings are preferred by publishers, the correct names of people and places, when to use italics and when not, the correct form of abbreviations, etc. - but not the meanings of words.

- *Roget's Thesaurus* - mine is the Penguin edition. It is easy to get too 'hooked' on the thesaurus - never using the obvious and simple word in the search for a different and perhaps more apposite word. Consult the thesaurus frequently - but ignore it often. Remember that the key to successful article-writing is simplicity of style.
- *The Gem Thesaurus* (Collins: London, 1964/77) - much smaller and easier to use than Roget's. Includes foreign nouns and a list of first names - in various languages.

- *Everyman's Dictionary of Quotations and Proverbs* (J. M. Dent: London 1951)
- *The Penguin Dictionary of Quotations* (Penguin Books: 1961)
- *The Penguin Dictionary of Modern Quotations* (Penguin Books: 1971)
- *Quotations for Our Times* (Magnum Books - Methuen: London, 1980)
- *A Dictionary of Contemporary Quotations* (Jonathon Green, Pan Books: London, 1982)
- *Chronological Dictionary of Quotations* (Edmund Wright, Bloomsbury: London, 1993)

Yes, half a dozen books - and with minimal overlap; if I see another modern one on sale I shall probably buy that too. Dictionaries of Quotations are marvellous source material for article-writers.

- *The Macmillan Encyclopedia* (Macmillan: London - updated annually)
- *The Collins Modern Encyclopedia* (Collins: London, 1969)
- *The Penguin Encyclopedia* (Penguin Books: 1965)

These three, well-thumbed, single-volume encyclopedia are my first source when starting research on a new subject. My next port of call is a special six-volume edition of Everyman's Encyclopedia. Quite often, I can obtain all I need from these sources: if not, I usually get an idea of where to look next.

## Writers' reference books

- *Writers' & Artists' Yearbook* (A. & C. Black: London, updated annually)
- *The Writer's Handbook* (Macmillan/PEN: London, updated annually)

No article-writer can afford to be without an up-to-date copy of one or other of these yearbooks; they cover an immense range of mainly British, but also overseas, publications and publishers. Because of their vast coverage, each yearbook entry offers only limited information. For more detailed information on a much smaller, select list of magazines, see my own ...

- *The Magazine Writer's Handbook* (Allison & Busby Writers' Guides: London, totally updated alternate years)

But not even my *Handbook* can obviate the need for every article-writer to do their own detailed market research - its purpose is more to 'take the edge off', to narrow the field for individual study.

Not actually about writing, but about meeting other writers; if you don't already belong to a writers' circle, consult the leading reference list (but remember the advice in Chapter 1, too):

- *The Directory of Writers' Circles*, Dick, Jill. (Laurence Pollinger Ltd: London.) Obtainable direct from Jill Dick, Oldacre, Horderns Park Road, Chapel-en-le-Frith, Derbyshire SK12 6SY - send a blank cheque, limited to £5, to cover cost plus postage (currently £4). This booklet lists just about every writers' organization in Britain - and is updated frequently.

## Books about writing style

- *The Complete Plain Words*, Gower, Sir Ernest (HMSO: London, 1973). 'The Bible'.
- *Good Grammar in One Hour*, King, Graham (Mandarin, in association with *The Sunday Times*: London, 1993). Free from

jargon; easy to read; and lives up to its 'one hour' claim.

- *The Technique of Clear Writing*, Gunning, Robert (McGraw-Hill: New York, 1968). Typical American 'hard-sell tuition' - full of good sense. Gunning is my own favourite guru. Mark Twain comes a close second - and third, is ...
- *Waterhouse on Newspaper Style*, Waterhouse, Keith (Viking: London, 1989, now also in Penguin paperback). Turn up no literary noses at this title: it is an excellent book about an effective and clear writing style ideal for article-writing for most markets. I cannot recommend it too highly.

## Books about 'the writing business'

- *How to Write Articles that Sell*, Wilbur, L. Perry (Wiley, New York, 1981). A particularly good book, but wholly oriented to the American market and American practices - which are still not quite the same as the British.
- *The Way to Write Magazine Articles* , Hines, John (Elm Tree Books - Hamish Hamilton: London, 1987). A different approach to mine but equally realistic.
- *Writers' Questions Answered*, Wells, Gordon (Allison & Busby Writers' Guides, London 1986). Whatever the question, the answer's probably here.
- *Research for Writers*, Hoffmann, Ann (A. & C. Black, London). A mine of information, aimed primarily at authors of non-fiction books but equally useful for all non-fiction writers; it explains in simple detail where to go for all sorts of information.

Next, a selection of books offering further, detailed advice about specific aspects of the craft of article-writing. I've read them all and learnt a lot from them.

- *How to Write Five-Minute Features*; Chisholm, Alison (Allison & Busby Writers' Guides, London, 1995)
- *How to Write Advertising Features,* Sheriff, John Paxton (Allison & Busby Writers' Guides, London, 1995)
- *How to Write and Sell Travel Articles*, Smith, Cathy (Allison & Busby Writers' Guides, London, 1992)

- *Photography for Article-Writers*, Wells, Gordon (Allison & Busby Writers' Guides, London, 1990)
- *How to Write and Sell Interviews*, Wright, Sally-Jayne (Allison & Busby Writers' Guides, London, 1995)

And, because many article-writers as they grow in competence, move on to writing a book ...

- *How to Write Non-Fiction Books*, Wells, Gordon (Allison & Busby Writers' Guides: London 1996). This is a new, updated and almost totally rewritten edition of my earlier book, *The Successful Author's Handbook* (Macmillan/Papermac: London, 1981/1989).

## Magazines about 'the writing business'

- *Writers' Monthly*, monthly, 29 Turnpike Lane, London N8 0EP. On subscription only. Tel: 0181-347 6778.
- *Writers News*, monthly, P.O. Box 4, Nairn IV12 4HU. On subscription only. Tel: 01667 454441.
- *Writing Magazine*, bi-monthly, from newsagents £1.80 per issue, or on subscription from *Writers News* as above.
- *Freelance Writing & Photography*, bi-monthly, Weavers Press Publishing Ltd, Clarendon Court, Over Wallop, Stockbridge, Hants SO20 8HU. On subscription only. Tel: 01264 782298.
- *Quartos*, bi-monthly, BCM-Writer, 27 Old Gloucester Street, London WC1N 3XX. On subscription only.
- *Writers' Forum*, quarterly, John Benton (editor/publisher), 9/10 Roberts Close, Moxley, Wednesbury, West Midlands WS10 8SS. On subscription only.

and a useful market study newsletter for writers - for keeping up to date with new publications, editorial wants, etc.

- *Freelance Market News*, monthly (eleven months a year), Freelance Press Services, Cumberland House, Lissadel Street, Salford M6 6GG. On subscription only. Tel: 0161-745 8850.

# INDEX